Build, Launch, and Sell a Real App with AI

A Hands-On Guide from Real Problem to First Customer

By Adam Seebeck

Copyright and Publication Information

A Hands-On Guide from Real Problem to First Customer

Adam Seebeck

unQbd Inc. 581 N Park Ave #4201 Apopka, FL 32704 USA

Print Year: 2026

This book provides educational information about product development and small business experiments. It does not provide legal, tax, accounting, financial, security, privacy, or accessibility advice. Rules and provider behavior vary by product, location, account, and date. Verify the requirements that apply before publishing, collecting information, accepting payment, or making a public claim.

AI systems can produce incorrect, incomplete, or unsafe output. Review generated work, protect private information, use bounded permissions, and verify important behavior before relying on it.

About unQbd

unQbd publishes practical books for modern readers. Explore books, audiobooks, and current reading options at https://unqbd.com/app.

About This Book

Who This Book Is For

This book is for a first-time builder who wants to turn a real problem into a small working app and a real business decision.

You do not need programming experience. You do not need a startup vocabulary, a business degree, or a finished idea.

You do need curiosity, access to an approved AI coding agent, and a willingness to test your assumptions.

An **AI coding agent** is a tool that can inspect project files, propose a plan, create software, run checks, and explain its work. Codex is one example. Other agents can fit when they support the same bounded workflow.

The agent handles implementation. You remain responsible for the problem, user, buyer, scope, permissions, proof, safety, offer, and next decision.

That division is the center of this book.

What You Will Build

You will build **Your App**. It begins with a problem you can observe in a person you can reach.

The first version stays small. One person should be able to enter the path, take the required action, and reach one useful result.

You will then watch someone use it. You will fix one observed barrier, test the trust boundaries, and state the limits that remain.

The final six chapters treat the app as a business. You will define one offer, one price hypothesis, one buyer path, one qualified audience, one bounded launch, and one decision rule.

The path can end with a purchase, commitment, refusal, or clean stop. The book does not promise a sale.

A first customer is possible. Honest evidence is required.

What You Will Not Learn

This is not a manual programming course.

You will not spend chapters memorizing Hypertext Markup Language, Cascading Style Sheets, or JavaScript syntax before you can build. The AI agent writes the implementation.

You will learn enough technical judgment to direct the work. You will decide what the app should do, what it should remember, which permissions it needs, and what evidence proves the result.

You will also learn when the first version has crossed into a larger risk. Accounts, sensitive data, custom payments, health decisions, legal rights, and shared private records require stronger review.

AI lowers the effort of creating software. It does not lower the consequence of being wrong.

The Builder Loop

Every chapter advances one part of the same method: the **Builder Loop**.

The loop moves from observation to definition, direction, proof, learning, and a human decision. It keeps the agent's speed connected to evidence.

Every meaningful agent task uses a four-part brief:

- **Goal:** the visible result you want.
- **Context:** the facts, files, evidence, and current behavior that matter.
- **Constraints:** the scope, permission, data, safety, and design limits.
- **Done when:** the checks that can pass or fail.

The brief is short on purpose. A narrow goal is easier to build, test, and reverse.

The detailed brief and agent procedure appear in Chapters 6 through 8. Later chapters reuse the procedure without turning the book into a programming manual.

Practice Loop and Your App

The book uses two clearly separated tracks.

Practice Loop is a constructed teaching case about an adult hobby learner. The app helps that person create one practice plan and later record what happened.

Every observation, conversation, price, cost, launch count, purchase, and usage number in the Practice Loop case is invented for instruction. None is unQbd research or live business evidence.

Practice Loop gives every reader the same facts to judge. You never build it.

Your App is the product you create from your own evidence. Its user, problem, promise, behavior, test results, offer, and decision should differ from the case.

Do not copy the case result into your own record. Copy the method.

The labels in the book make the difference clear. `Practice Loop` introduces the constructed example. `Do It for Your App` applies the move to your project.

One Result Per Chapter

The book has twenty short chapters. Each chapter creates one result that feeds the next.

1. **Broken Moment:** one repeated moment, visible cost, and current method.
2. **Problem Snapshot:** one first user and a problem claim with visible assumptions.
3. **Buyer Map:** the user, buyer, approver, and operator roles.
4. **Evidence Decision:** brief, investigate, change, or stop based on real behavior and a next step.
5. **Outcome Promise:** one result the user can recognize.
6. **Build Brief:** the goal, context, constraints, states, data, checks, and exclusions.

7. **Agent Work Order:** the inspect, plan, implement, test, report, and decision cycle.
8. **Scope Box:** what is inside now, manual for this test, or later or never.
9. **Working Path:** one complete route from empty state to useful result and safe exit.
10. **Data Decision:** what the app forgets, keeps on one device, or places behind an account.
11. **Observation Note:** what a relevant person did, said, and what you inferred.
12. **Change Decision:** one observed barrier, bounded fix, retest, and keep, revise, revert, or stop.
13. **Trust Map:** what enters, stays, leaves, who can act, and what the product claims.
14. **Recovery Plan:** the safe next action, message, proof, and owner for important failures.
15. **Offer One-Pager:** the buyer, result, product, help, limits, price hypothesis, and next action.
16. **Buyer Path:** discovery, understanding, decision, payment or inquiry, delivery, use, support, and removal.
17. **Audience List:** the smallest eligible, reachable group that can act on the offer.
18. **Launch Log:** reached, replies, decisions, purchases, delivery, use, time, and cost kept separate.
19. **Business Scorecard:** problem, product, offer, path, and economics read as separate evidence lanes.
20. **Founder Decision:** continue, change, or stop with one constraint and a fixed next rule.

You do not need a perfect result in every chapter. A failed or unproven check is useful when you record it honestly.

How to Use the Book

Read the chapters in order. Each one assumes that the previous result exists.

Do the work for Your App before moving on. Keep the app, control files, checkpoints, and business records in one project folder.

Ask the agent to maintain routine logs and changed-file reports. Review every statement that changes a user, claim, permission, feature, price, cost, or decision.

Run the app yourself. A confident agent report is not proof.

Use non-sensitive information during development and testing. Keep passwords, private keys, payment credentials, customer records, school records, health information, and private conversations out of prompts.

Stop before any action that publishes, sends, spends, charges, deletes outside the project, or connects a private account. Confirm the exact action and owner first.

The retail chapters contain the full method. A separate lab companion adds timing, detailed prompts, evidence checklists, and course safeguards.

In the high-school cohort, the teaching meeting covers one two-chapter pair. The second meeting is a lab that produces the paired results. Ten weeks still cover the complete twenty-chapter book.

If You Are Under 18

You can complete the product and business decisions in this book without owning a public account or taking money.

A parent, guardian, school, or instructor approves the AI tool, device access, outside participants, contact method, public route, payment, refund, and customer-support process.

Do not privately contact unknown adults. Do not publish your school, age, photo, hometown, email address, phone number, or another direct contact detail.

In the high-school cohort, use only the local, preview, outreach, and publishing route approved for that program. An approved adult owns any transaction and public communication.

When approval is unavailable, keep the work local. Mark the outside step unproven instead of bypassing the boundary.

What Counts as Success

Success is not a large feature list.

Success is a completed path and a decision supported by evidence.

You may finish with one paying customer. You may learn that the offer needs a change. You may stop because the problem, buyer, economics, risk, or your priorities no longer support the work.

All three outcomes can be responsible.

The weak outcome is a polished app attached to a story you never tested.

Start with Chapter 1. Find the problem before asking AI to build the solution.

Table of Contents

Part I: Find a Problem That Matters

Chapter 1: Start with a Broken Moment

The Move

Start with one moment that keeps going wrong.

When I started unQbd, pronounced "uncubed," I was looking at a reading experience that had been split into pieces.

You could buy a book on Amazon. If you wanted the audiobook, you went to Audible. If you wanted conversation, you went to Goodreads. If that story became a show, you searched a streaming service or YouTube.

Each piece lived somewhere else. The pieces did not know about one another.

That was the problem I kept coming back to. Books were treated as isolated products, but readers moved between reading, listening, watching, and talking.

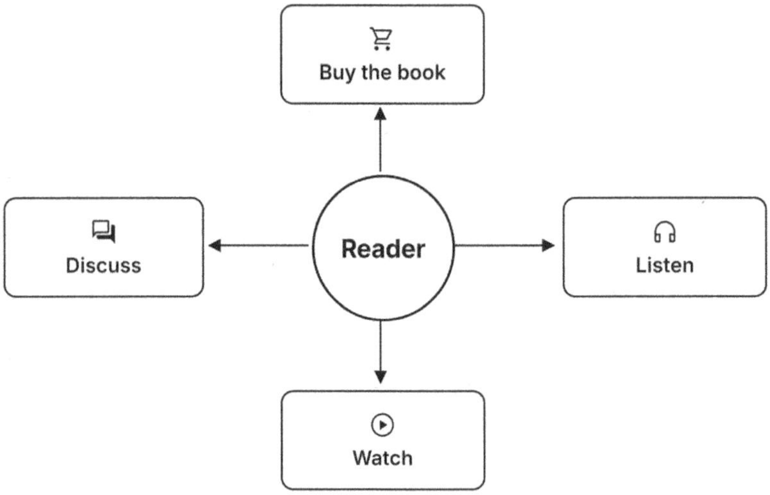

One story. Four disconnected experiences.

I did not begin with a complete platform plan. I began with a moment that felt broken.

That distinction matters. "Build a reading platform" is a solution. "A reader leaves the book to find every other part of the experience" is a problem.

Your first job is not to name an app. Your job is to describe one moment clearly enough that another person can recognize it.

Use this sentence:

> *When **this person** tries to **do this, this friction** keeps happening, so **this cost** follows.*

Your result is one **Broken Moment**. It will become the first half of your Problem Snapshot in Chapter 2.

Why It Matters

AI can build the wrong idea very quickly.

That sounds obvious, but it changes the starting point. Building used to require enough time and skill that many weak ideas never became products. Now a vague idea can become a polished screen before anyone asks whether it should exist.

Fast building does not rescue a weak problem. It hides the weakness behind a better-looking product.

This is why the book uses the **Builder Loop**:

1. **Observe:** find out what actually happens.
2. **Define:** choose the problem and the next result.
3. **Direct:** give the agent a bounded job.
4. **Prove:** check the result against the brief.
5. **Learn:** separate what the evidence shows from what you assumed.
6. **Decide:** choose whether to continue, change, or stop.

You will use this loop at different sizes, from one interface change to a business decision. This chapter starts with Observe.

A useful broken moment has five parts:

1. **A trigger:** something starts the moment.
2. **An action:** the person tries to make progress.
3. **Friction:** something slows, blocks, confuses, or repeats.
4. **A visible cost:** time, money, effort, uncertainty, delay, or lost information follows.
5. **A current method:** the person does something today, even if that method is awkward.

The current method is important because most problems do not sit untouched. People use notes, messages, spreadsheets, memory, paper, or another product. A workaround tells you the person cares enough to act.

It can also tell you the problem is already solved.

Imagine someone says, "Planning is annoying." That is a complaint, not yet a broken moment.

Now make it concrete:

> *When I return to a plan I wrote earlier, I cannot tell which version is current, so I spend ten minutes rebuilding work I already did.*

The second version gives you behavior and cost. It also gives you something to observe.

Do not make the problem sound larger than it is. Small, repeated friction can support a useful product. A giant mission statement can hide the fact that no single moment has been chosen.

The early unQbd problem becomes clearer when written as behavior:

> *When a reader wants to continue one story in another format, the reader leaves the current experience, searches elsewhere, and starts over with another account or service.*

That statement does not prove a market. It does not prove people will pay unQbd. It only names a moment worth examining.

This is the right standard for your first chapter too.

Avoid three common shortcuts.

Shortcut 1: Starting with a feature

"I want an AI dashboard" names a feature. It does not say who needs it or what fails without it.

Shortcut 2: Starting with a category

"People need a productivity app" names a market category. It does not show a repeated action or cost.

Shortcut 3: Starting with your own excitement

You are allowed to be excited. Excitement gets you moving. It does not count as evidence that someone else has the same problem.

The Broken Moment keeps those ideas honest. It is not a final verdict. It is the first claim you will try to disprove.

Three places broken moments hide

Many useful problems appear at a handoff.

One tool ends before the person's job ends. Information moves from email to a spreadsheet, from a meeting to a task list, or from a book to another format. The person has to carry the context across the gap.

The original unQbd problem is a handoff problem. The story continues, but the reader must leave one product and reconstruct the experience somewhere else.

Other problems appear through repetition.

The person copies the same answer, rebuilds the same list, checks the same status, or explains the same context every time. Repeated work does not always need software. It does deserve inspection.

A third group appears when state is lost.

The person knows what was supposed to happen but cannot tell what did happen. A note preserves an intention but not the result. A request was sent, but no one can tell who answered. A file exists, but no one knows whether it is current.

Look for these three patterns:

- **Handoff:** the work crosses a gap between tools, people, or formats.
- **Repetition:** the same useful action must be rebuilt.
- **Lost state:** the person cannot tell what is current, complete, approved, or true.

They are not product categories. They are places to observe.

Frequency, cost, and consequence

A problem does not need to score high on every measure.

A small problem that happens every day can matter. A rare problem with a large consequence can matter. A frequent problem with no meaningful cost may remain an annoyance.

Write all three separately:

```
How often the moment occurs:

What one occurrence costs:

What happens if nothing changes:
```

Do not multiply guesses into a dramatic total. If you do not know the frequency, write `unknown`. The unknown becomes part of the evidence work.

This keeps you from turning one frustrating afternoon into a universal claim. It also keeps you from dismissing a quiet problem that steadily consumes time or trust.

A broad vision can start with a narrow break

The original unQbd vision is broader than one handoff. It connects reading, listening, watching, and conversation. That broader vision helps explain where the company may go.

It still does not change the first product question.

If I try to solve every part at once, I must decide about content rights, accounts, media, social behavior, devices, payments, and discovery. That happens before I know which broken moment matters most.

The vision should guide the direction. The Broken Moment should control the next move.

Use that distinction for your app:

```
Broader vision:

One broken moment inside that vision:

What I am deliberately not solving yet:
```

You do not betray the vision by narrowing the start. You make the first claim small enough to observe, challenge, and improve.

Practice Loop

Practice Loop is a constructed teaching case used throughout this book. It is not a real unQbd product, customer study, or sales result.

The case begins with an adult hobby learner who writes practice plans in a notes app.

One note says what the person intended to practice. Days later, the note is still there, but it does not show whether the practice happened or what the result was.

The broken moment is:

> *When an adult hobby learner returns to an unstructured practice note, the original intention is visible but the result is missing, so the learner cannot tell what actually happened.*

That looks promising because the behavior repeats and information is lost.

Then the case adds a counterexample. Another learner uses a dated paper log with a completion mark. That person can tell what happened.

The counterexample matters. It shows that "people cannot track practice" is too broad. Some people already have a working method.

The case has not earned an app yet. It has only earned a narrower question about people whose current method preserves intention but not outcome.

Do It for Your App

Start with a frustration you have seen, experienced, or can reach directly.

Do not search for the most impressive idea. Search for a moment you can describe without guessing.

Write short answers to these prompts:

```
Person in the moment:

What starts the moment:

What the person tries to do:

What keeps going wrong:

Visible cost:

Current method:

What I am still assuming:

BROKEN MOMENT
When __________ tries to __________, __________ keeps happening,
so __________ follows.
```

Now turn the answers into the final sentence at the bottom of the same record.

Keep the sentence free of solution words when possible. Words such as app, dashboard, platform, marketplace, automation, and AI often drag you into a product too early.

Compare these examples.

Weak:

> *Small businesses need an AI app for customer service.*

Stronger:

> *When a solo business owner receives the same basic question in several places, the owner rewrites the answer each time, so replies are delayed and work is repeated.*

Weak:

> *Students need a better planner.*

Stronger:

> *When a student receives assignments in several systems, one deadline is copied incorrectly, so the student works from an incomplete list.*

The stronger versions are not automatically good businesses. They can be tested.

Next, look for a current method. The solo owner may use saved replies. The student may use a paper calendar. Those methods can become competitors, evidence, or proof that no new product is needed.

Do not hide counterevidence. If the current method works well, record that. A problem that disappears under inspection should stop the build before it consumes more time.

Finally, name the cost without exaggeration. "This ruins everything" is rarely useful. "This adds ten minutes," "this creates a missed deadline," or "this leaves the result unknown" gives you something you can check.

Before you finish, read the Broken Moment without the cost phrase. If the problem still sounds exactly the same, the cost is probably too vague.

Then check the notes behind the sentence. They should name the current method and explain where it falls short. The sentence alone does not need every detail.

The two details keep the statement grounded. They also give you a clean way to be wrong. If thc cost is smaller than expected or the current method works, the idea should shrink or stop.

Prove It

Your Broken Moment passes this chapter when:

- it names one person in one situation;
- it describes behavior rather than a feature;
- the friction repeats or has a meaningful cost;
- the current method is visible; and
- at least one assumption is still labeled as an assumption.

If you cannot pass those checks, do not ask AI to build anything yet. Rewrite the moment until another person could recognize or reject it.

Your Result

Save the one-sentence **Broken Moment** and the seven short notes behind it.

In Chapter 2, you will choose the first person whose real behavior can test whether this moment deserves more attention.

Chapter 2: Choose One Person

The Move

Choose the first person, not the largest audience.

unQbd can serve many kinds of readers. That is true at the company level. It is not useful at the start of one product decision.

"People who like books" includes a parent choosing a picture book, a developer buying a technical guide, a fiction reader listening during a commute, and a student joining a course.

Those people do not enter with the same problem. They do not choose the same product for the same reason.

When I narrow the early unQbd problem, the first useful person is not "everyone who reads." It is a reader in a specific moment, such as someone who wants to continue one story in another format without rebuilding the experience elsewhere.

That does not make the company small. It makes the decision clear.

Your move is to choose one person whose behavior can confirm or reject the Broken Moment from Chapter 1.

Your result is one **First User** description. It will complete your Problem Snapshot.

Why It Matters

A broad audience feels safer because it keeps every possibility open.

In practice, it weakens the product.

If your first user is "busy people," every feature can sound reasonable. Reminders, calendars, sharing, automation, analytics, mobile access, and AI summaries all fit someone in that group.

The product becomes a pile of possible needs.

A useful First User description contains five things:

1. **Situation:** what is happening when the problem appears.
2. **Behavior:** what the person actually does now.
3. **Current method:** the tool, habit, or workaround already in use.
4. **Constraint:** what makes the moment difficult for this person.
5. **Reachability:** how you can observe or speak with someone who fits.

Notice what is missing. You do not need a fictional name, favorite coffee, personality type, or long life story.

Demographics matter only when they change the product, buying authority, safety, or access. Age matters when an adult must approve an account or payment. Location matters when the product depends on local availability. Job title matters when authority or workflow changes with the role.

Otherwise, behavior is usually more useful.

Compare these descriptions.

Too broad:

> *People who want to be more organized.*

Useful:

> *A volunteer club organizer who receives attendance replies through text and email, then rebuilds the list before every meeting.*

The useful description creates an observable moment. You can watch how the list is made. You can see whether the current method works. You can find out whether the cost is annoying or meaningful.

Specificity also protects you from false agreement.

Someone outside the moment can still like your idea. That opinion does not tell you whether the product fits the person who has the problem.

Choose reachability over imagination. A modest problem you can inspect is a stronger starting point than a dramatic problem belonging to people you cannot reach.

You do not need hundreds of people. You need enough access to learn whether your description matches reality before the build grows.

The first user is not a permanent market boundary. It is the first honest place to learn.

Move down the specificity ladder

Start broad if that is how the idea arrived. Then narrow it one level at a time.

For example:

1. people who organize events;
2. volunteer organizers;
3. volunteer organizers preparing recurring meetings;
4. volunteer organizers who receive attendance changes through several message threads; and
5. volunteer organizers who rebuild one attendance list before each recurring meeting.

The final description is not automatically better because it is longer. It is better because the situation, behavior, method, and failure are visible.

Stop narrowing when another person can answer two questions:

- Does this description fit me?
- Can I show you the last time it happened?

If the answer to both is no, the description is still too vague or aimed at the wrong person.

Reachable is not the same as representative

Your first three reachable people do not represent an entire market. They give you a place to learn.

Friends and family can be useful when they genuinely perform the behavior. They are poor evidence when they are included only because they are available.

Use this check:

Reachable person	Has the real behavior?	Can show the current method?	Useful for this test?
Person A	Yes	Yes	Yes
Person B	No	No	No, even if supportive
Person C	Yes	Not yet	Maybe, after the method is verified

The point is not to reject helpful people. It is to keep encouragement separate from problem evidence.

Do not confuse a first user with an edge case

Specificity should reveal the center of the first problem, not the most unusual version.

If one person has ten special requirements that no one else shares, building for that person can turn the product into custom work. Look for repeated behavior that several reachable people can recognize.

The first user should be narrow enough to observe and common enough to find again.

That balance matters later. You will need more than one person to test the product and more than one eligible buyer to test the offer.

Use behavior without turning it into a stereotype

A narrow user is not a collection of assumptions about a type of person.

Suppose you choose parents planning groceries. That label alone does not tell you who writes the list, who shops, or how additions arrive. It also does not tell you whether the household already has a method that works.

Write the behavior you actually need:

> *A household shopper who writes the grocery list before leaving home, then receives additions by text while shopping.*

Now the description changes the product without pretending every parent shops the same way.

"Busy parent," "small-business owner," and "retiree" can hide more than they reveal. Ask which behavior, constraint, authority, or current method makes the problem appear.

Run a removal check on every detail:

```
If I remove this detail, does the problem, product, safety, buying
authority,
or reach path change?
```

If nothing changes, remove the detail. The goal is not to describe the whole person. It is to describe the part of the situation your next decision must understand.

Practice Loop

Practice Loop begins with four constructed adult hobby learners.

Two use unstructured methods:

- one writes practice plans in a notes app and later cannot tell what happened; and
- one dismisses calendar reminders and later cannot remember whether the session occurred.

Two have working alternatives:

- one uses a dated paper log with a completion mark; and
- one uses an instructor's existing tracker with an outcome status.

The first user is not "anyone who practices a skill."

The narrower description is:

> *An adult hobby learner who uses unstructured notes or reminders, repeatedly preserves the practice intention, and later cannot distinguish the plan from the result.*

The current method and the failure belong together. The two people with working systems remain counterevidence, not targets waiting to be persuaded.

This is a constructed case. The four records are supplied for instruction. They are not a market sample or forecast.

Do It for Your App

Return to your Broken Moment and choose the person most closely connected to it.

Complete this description:

```
My first user is:

The problem appears when:

This person currently:

The current method fails because:

The important constraint is:

I can reach or observe this person through:

People I am not targeting yet:
```

The final line is useful. A clear exclusion keeps a later conversation from widening the product.

Suppose your original idea is a shared shopping tool.

"Families" is too broad. One possible First User is:

> *A person planning groceries for a two-adult household who receives additions through text after the list has already been written.*

That person, moment, and current method are concrete. A restaurant buyer, roommate group, and parent managing five schedules may have related problems, but they are not the same first test.

Now test your reachability.

In private notes, identify three real people or three real places where this behavior occurs. Use anonymous labels in any record you share with the agent. You do not need to contact anyone in this chapter. You are checking whether your chosen person exists within reach.

If every route depends on strangers replying to cold outreach, the problem may still be real, but it is a difficult first learning environment.

If you are under 18, use people you already know and follow the approval rules in your course or household. Do not contact unknown adults or create public accounts to complete this step.

Then check whether the constraint changes the product.

Examples:

- weak internet access changes whether the app can depend on a constant connection;
- shared devices change privacy and sign-out behavior;
- a buyer who is not the user changes the offer;
- local service availability changes whether location belongs in the product; and
- sensitive information changes what should never be collected.

Do not solve those issues yet. Record them so they cannot hide later.

Finally, remove any detail that does not change the problem, product, evidence, or reachability. A short accurate description is better than a vivid fictional profile.

Write one sentence explaining why this person comes first:

```
This person comes first because I can observe the real behavior,
inspect the current method, and test one result without adding
another audience.
```

If that sentence is not true, choose someone closer to the evidence. The best first user is not the person who makes the market sound largest. It is the person who makes the next decision most honest.

Prove It

Your First User passes this chapter when:

- the person is defined by a real situation and behavior;
- the current method is named;
- one meaningful constraint is visible;
- at least three reachable examples or locations exist; and
- adjacent audiences are explicitly deferred.

If the person exists only in your imagination, go back to Chapter 1 and choose a moment closer to you.

Your Result

Combine the Broken Moment and First User into one **Problem Snapshot**.

In Chapter 3, you will identify who uses the product, who pays, and who must approve the decision. Those roles may belong to one person or several.

Chapter 3: Name the User and the Buyer

The Move

Separate the person who uses the product from the person who can say yes.

At unQbd, those roles change with the product.

An adult developer buying one of my technical books can be the user, buyer, and approver. The same person sees the need, chooses the book, pays, and reads it.

A children's product is different. A child may use the experience, while a parent chooses it, pays for it, and approves the account or public activity.

A course for high school students creates another split. The student does the work. The parent may be the buyer and must approve accounts, payments, outside contact, and publication.

If I speak only to the user, I can miss the person who controls the decision. If I speak only to the buyer, I can create an offer that sounds sensible but fails during use.

Your move is to name the roles before you design the product or offer.

Your result is one **Buyer Map**.

Why It Matters

The word customer often hides several jobs.

Use four roles:

- **User:** completes the product action and experiences the result.
- **Buyer:** accepts the exchange and pays or commits resources.
- **Approver:** has authority to permit the action, account, payment, or risk.

- **Operator:** delivers, supports, and fixes the product.

In a small consumer app, the same person often uses, buys, and approves. You, the builder, usually remain the operator.

The roles can also split.

Someone else may influence the choice without owning it. An instructor's recommendation can matter, but it does not give the instructor payment or approval authority. Note that influence beside the relevant role when it affects the decision.

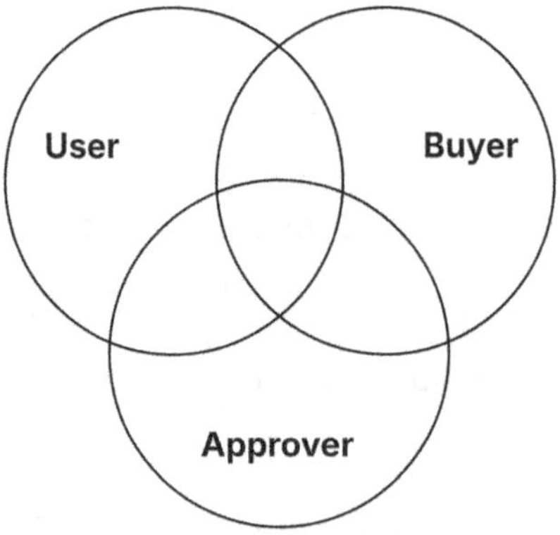

Independent adult: one person can hold all three roles.

Student product: the roles may be split.

Consider a tool that helps an employee prepare a weekly report. The employee may use it. A manager may approve it. A company may pay. The builder may support it.

Each role needs different proof.

The user needs to believe the product will make the moment better. The buyer needs to understand the value and price. The approver needs to understand risk and control. The operator needs to know that delivery and support are manageable.

A product can work for one role and fail for another.

The user may love a feature that requires data the approver will not allow. The buyer may like the price while the user refuses the workflow. The operator may discover that every sale creates an hour of manual setup.

You do not need to solve every role now. You do need to know which role must say yes before the next step can happen.

Start with the simplest honest arrangement.

If the user can also buy and approve, keep the first test there. A split-role product can still be worth building, but it creates more evidence work.

Do not pretend the roles are shared when they are not. A child cannot become the payment owner because it makes the first offer easier. An employee may not have authority to connect a work account. A patient may not be able to approve a clinical claim.

Authority is part of the product.

The Buyer Map also changes your language.

The user hears a product promise: what can I do?

The buyer hears an offer: what do I receive for the price?

The approver hears a responsibility question: what can happen, and how is it controlled?

When those answers disagree, the product is not ready.

Four mismatches to catch early

The Buyer Map is useful because it exposes mismatch before a polished product makes the mismatch harder to see.

Product mismatch happens when the user needs one result and the buyer purchases another promise. A manager may buy reporting visibility while the employee expects less reporting work. The same feature can feel helpful to one and intrusive to the other.

Value mismatch happens when the product works but the buyer does not value the result enough to pay. A user can enjoy a free tool without accepting a paid offer.

Authority mismatch happens when the person saying yes cannot approve the account, data connection, payment, or public use. Enthusiasm without authority does not move the product forward.

Operating mismatch happens when every success creates more support than the builder can deliver. The buyer sees a simple purchase. The operator sees setup, questions, corrections, refunds, and recovery.

Write these mismatches down while the product is still small. They are cheaper to change on paper.

The buyer is not an obstacle

Builders sometimes treat the buyer or approver as a gate standing between the product and the "real" user.

That framing creates bad products.

The buyer may know something important about budget, timing, or alternatives. The approver may carry responsibility the user does not. A parent approving a child's account is not friction to remove. The approval is part of a safe product.

Your job is not to work around a required role. Your job is to make the value, limits, and controls understandable to that role.

When one person holds every role, keep the language simple. When roles split, the product and offer must make the handoffs visible.

Trace one decision all the way through

Role maps become easier when you follow one real decision instead of discussing the product in general.

Choose the next action you want, such as:

- join a test;
- create an account;
- connect data;
- make a purchase;
- approve publication; or

- receive ongoing support.

Then ask who must act at each handoff.

For the high-school cohort, a student may decide to participate, but that decision does not automatically authorize payment, outside contact, a public app, or a live account. The parent or program can own those decisions while the student still owns the learning and product work.

For an adult buying a technical book, the path can be simpler. The same person may discover the book, judge the topic, approve the price, pay, and read.

Complete one decision trace:

```
Action we want next:
Person who experiences the result:
Person who pays or commits resources:
Person who must approve:
Person who delivers or supports:
First role that can stop the path:
Information that role needs:
```

If a required role cannot be reached, the problem may still be real. The current offer is not ready. Record the missing handoff instead of asking the user to act beyond their authority.

Practice Loop

In this constructed case, Practice Loop chooses an adult hobby learner as the first user.

For the first test, the same adult is also the buyer and approver. That keeps the initial exchange simple.

The map is:

Role	First case choice	What must be true
User	Adult hobby learner	The practice intention and outcome gap is real for this person.
Buyer	Same adult	The person understands the offer and chooses whether it is worth the price.
Approver	Same adult	The person can approve participation, local data, contact, and any later purchase.
Operator	Case builder	Setup and support stay inside the written limit.

A parent, instructor, or coach could become a buyer in a later version. That possibility is not evidence.

Adding one of those roles would change the product. A parent may want visibility. An instructor may want several learners. Those requests could create accounts, permissions, dashboards, and sensitive records.

The constructed case defers them. The first buyer remains the adult user. These role choices are teaching inputs, not real customer evidence.

Do It for Your App

Create a Buyer Map for the First User from Chapter 2.

Use this table:

```
USER
Who uses the product:
What useful result this person needs:
What could make this person refuse:

BUYER
Who pays or commits resources:
What value this person needs to understand:
What could make this person refuse:

APPROVER
Who must permit the account, data, payment, or risk:
What control this person needs:
What could make this person refuse:

OPERATOR
Who delivers and supports the product:
What work each successful use creates:
What limit keeps the work manageable:
```

If the same person holds several roles, write that clearly. Do not invent separate people to make the map look complete.

Then mark the first required yes.

For a direct consumer tool, the user's yes may be enough to run a free test. A payment still requires the buyer's yes. A public account or outside contact may require another approver.

For a product used inside a school, company, or regulated setting, approval may come before use.

If the product involves a minor, money, sensitive information, health, legal decisions, or physical safety, treat authority as a design constraint. Do not work around it.

Now compare the promise for each role.

Suppose the product helps a volunteer organizer build one attendance list from several message threads.

The organizer as user may value less copying. The club treasurer as buyer may care about price. The club leader as approver may care about member information. The builder as operator may care about how many message formats require manual cleanup.

One simple idea now has four acceptance tests.

That is useful. The map has exposed the real decision before software hides it.

Finally, decide whether the first version can use one person in all primary roles. If not, keep the split and accept that the evidence plan in Chapter 4 must include more than the user.

You can also write one refusal statement for each role:

```
The user should refuse if:

The buyer should refuse if:

The approver should refuse if:

The operator should stop delivery if:
```

This is not negative copy. It is boundary work.

For example, the buyer should refuse if the offer claims a result the product has not proved. The approver should refuse if the product collects information without a clear reason or deletion path. The operator should stop if delivery requires access or responsibility outside the written offer.

A good first product makes a qualified yes easier and an unqualified yes harder.

Prove It

Your Buyer Map passes this chapter when:

- the user and buyer are named separately, even if they are the same person;
- every required approver is visible;
- the operator and support limit are named;
- each role has one reason to accept and one reason to refuse; and
- no person is given authority that person does not have.

Your Result

Save the **Buyer Map** beside your Problem Snapshot.

In Chapter 4, you will collect only the evidence needed to decide whether this problem, person, and buyer deserve a small build.

Chapter 4: Prove the Problem Before You Build

The Move

Earn the build with behavior, not compliments.

I can learn something useful when a technical book sells. The sale supports that title, topic, price, and buyer decision.

It does not prove that the buyer wants an all-in-one reading platform. It does not prove that the buyer will subscribe. It does not prove that the next unQbd feature should exist.

The evidence has a boundary.

Founders get into trouble when one encouraging signal is asked to prove five different things.

Your move is to decide what evidence would justify one small build, then look for that evidence before you open the coding agent.

Your result is one **Evidence Decision**: brief, investigate, change, or stop. Brief means the evidence earns a Build Brief for one small prototype.

Why It Matters

Evidence becomes stronger when it costs the other person something real.

Use this ladder from weak to strong:

1. **Compliment:** "That sounds useful."
2. **Stated frustration:** the person says the problem is annoying.
3. **Repeated behavior:** the same failure has happened more than once.
4. **Visible cost or working alternative:** time, money, effort, risk, or an existing solution is visible.

5. **Committed next step:** the person agrees to a specific action, such as a scheduled test, data review, deposit, or purchase.

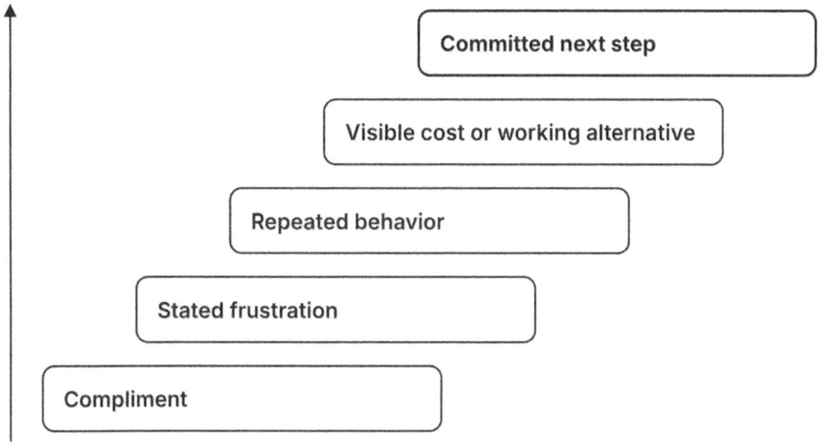

Match the size of the decision to the strength of the evidence.

The ladder does not mean a purchase is required before every prototype. It means the size of your next step should match the strength of the evidence.

A compliment can justify another question. Repeated behavior can justify a sketch. A committed test can justify a small local prototype. A real purchase can justify delivery work.

Do not jump three levels.

Past behavior is usually more useful than future intention.

"Would you use this?" asks the person to imagine a future and often rewards politeness.

"Tell me about the last time this happened" asks for a real event.

Use questions like these:

- What happened the last time?
- What did you do next?
- How often has that happened recently?
- What did it cost in time, money, effort, or uncertainty?

- What do you use now?
- What works well about the current method?
- What would make you refuse a test?

Do not pitch between questions. The purpose is to learn what is true, not to win agreement.

Working alternatives are especially valuable.

If paper solves the problem, paper is not an obstacle to overcome. It is evidence that your product must be meaningfully better for a specific person.

Counterevidence protects you from building around your own excitement. Record it beside the supportive evidence. Do not move it into a footnote.

Set the decision rule before the conversations. Otherwise, you will be tempted to change the rule after hearing the answer.

A first decision rule can be modest:

> *Build one local prototype only if three relevant people describe the repeated problem and at least one schedules a short test.*

That rule does not estimate a market. It controls your next investment.

The goal is not certainty. The goal is an evidence level appropriate to a small, reversible build.

What each signal earns

Different signals earn different actions.

Signal	What it may earn	What it does not prove
Compliment	Another question	Use, purchase, or urgency
Repeated behavior	A clearer problem statement	Willingness to change
Visible cost	A small test of a better path	Willingness to pay
Working alternative	A product standard or stop decision	That your version will win
Scheduled test	A bounded prototype	Demand at scale
Purchase	Delivery to that buyer	Retention or a repeatable business

This table protects the next decision from ambition.

One scheduled test is valuable because the person commits time. It is still one scheduled test. One purchase is meaningful because an exchange occurred. It is still one buyer.

Use the signal fully, but do not ask it to carry a larger claim.

Evidence can change the product before the build

Good evidence does more than say yes or no.

It can narrow the person, change the promise, expose a working alternative, or reveal that the buyer and user are different.

Suppose three people describe the problem, but all three solve it by sending one message to a trusted person. The opportunity may be a service or a clearer handoff, not an app.

Suppose the problem repeats, but no one will schedule a ten-minute test. The friction may be real and unimportant.

Suppose the person will test, but only if the product stores sensitive information you are not prepared to protect. The right decision may be stop.

Evidence is not a vote on your original idea. It is permission to change the idea before code creates attachment.

Keep the conversation clean

Do not lead with a demo. Do not explain why the current method is bad. Do not rescue a weak answer by describing more features.

Ask for the last event, then remain quiet long enough to hear the sequence.

If the person cannot remember the last event, record that. If the current method works, record that. If the person changes the subject, do not convert the new topic into support for the old problem.

Clean evidence can disappoint you and still save the project.

Decide what a no will save

A stop rule becomes easier to respect when you name the cost it protects.

Before collecting evidence, write what happens if the rule fails:

```
If the problem does not repeat, I will save:

If no relevant person takes the next step, I will avoid building:

If the required data or responsibility is too high, I will stop
before:
```

This is not pessimism. It is investment control.

A no before the build can save weeks of product work. A no before live payment can save support and refund problems. A no before sensitive data can save a responsibility the product was never ready to carry.

The evidence can also earn a smaller yes than you expected. If the decision rule supports a sketch but not a coded prototype, run the sketch. If it supports one scheduled test but not public launch, build only for that test.

The Evidence Decision should release one specific next investment. It should not release every future stage.

Practice Loop

Practice Loop uses four constructed adult hobby learner records.

Before reviewing them, the case builder writes this rule:

> *Build one local prototype only if at least two of four relevant adults describe a repeated intention-to-outcome gap, and at least one schedules a local test.*

The records are:

Record	Past behavior	Current method	Next step
A	Two recent notes preserve a plan but not the result.	Notes app	Schedules a twenty-minute local test.
B	A dated log shows both plan and completion.	Paper log	Declines the test because the method works.
C	Two reminders were dismissed, and the outcomes are unknown.	Calendar reminders and memory	Schedules a twenty-minute local test.
D	An existing tracker records the outcome.	Instructor's app	Declines the test because the method works.

The case passes its narrow rule.

It does not prove that all hobby learners have the problem. It does not prove demand, price, or purchase intent. It supports one local prototype for adults using unstructured notes or reminders.

Records B and D remain important. They narrow the target and show what a working outcome record looks like.

This is constructed teaching data, not unQbd research or a forecast.

Do It for Your App

Write your decision rule before collecting evidence.

```
I will prepare a Build Brief for one small local prototype only if:

Repeated behavior required:

Visible cost or failed current method required:

Committed next step required:

I will investigate further if:

I will choose another problem or first user if:

I will stop if:

DECISION: Brief | Investigate | Change '| Stop

THIS DECISION DOES NOT YET PROVE

NEXT EVIDENCE REQUIRED AFTER THE PROTOTYPE
```

Keep the rule proportional. You are not raising a large investment round. You are deciding whether a small build deserves time.

Now choose the evidence method.

For most first products, use a combination of:

- a short conversation about the last real event;
- observation of the current method;
- review of an existing artifact, such as a note, form, or spreadsheet; and
- a specific invitation to test the smallest possible result.

Ask permission before viewing another person's information. Remove private details from your notes. Do not paste private conversations or personal data into an AI prompt.

If you are under 18, use people you already know and an approved adult process. Do not contact unknown adults, promise payment, or create public research forms without approval.

Keep a simple evidence table:

```
Person or anonymous label:
Relevant situation:
What happened last time:
Current method:
What works:
What fails:
Visible cost:
Counterevidence:
Committed next step:
```

After the evidence is collected, apply the original rule without rewriting it.

Choose one decision:

Brief

The required behavior and next step are present. Prepare a brief for the smallest prototype needed for the scheduled test. Chapters 6 through 8 define and check its boundaries before implementation.

Investigate

The problem may be real, but reachability, authority, evidence, or timing is too weak. Name the missing signal and when you will check again.

Change

The evidence points to a different problem or first user. Return to Chapters 1 and 2 and revise the Problem Snapshot before collecting more evidence.

Stop

The current method works, the problem does not repeat, the cost is too small, or the required responsibility is too high for this project.

Stopping is not failure. It is the cheapest successful use of the method.

Write the conclusion at the same size as the evidence.

Do not write "the market wants this" after four conversations. Write "this evidence supports one local test with this person under these limits."

That sentence gives the AI agent a safer job later.

Complete the two evidence-limit lines beneath the decision. The first prevents a local test from becoming a market claim. The second keeps the next chapter connected to learning instead of feature growth.

Prove It

Your Evidence Decision passes this chapter when:

- the decision rule was written before the evidence was judged;
- past behavior and the current method are recorded;
- counterevidence is preserved;
- one committed next step or its absence is visible; and
- the conclusion supports only the next small investment.

Your Result

Save the **Evidence Decision** with brief, investigate, change, or stop selected.

If the decision is brief, Chapter 5 will turn the evidence into one narrow promise. If it is investigate, collect the missing evidence before proceeding. If it is change, revise the Problem Snapshot. If it is stop, close this idea without building it.

Part II: Give AI a Clear Job

Chapter 5: Make One Narrow Promise

The Move

Promise one result the first product can honestly create.

With unQbd, I have a broad direction: Read. Listen. Watch. Connect.

That line helps explain why the company exists. It does not tell an AI agent what to build first. It also does not tell one reader what must happen during one product session.

A large direction needs smaller product promises inside it.

If a reader opens one book, a narrow promise might concern finding the related audio or continuing the same story. It should not claim that every book, format, device, and community experience is already connected.

The same rule applies to your app.

Use the evidence from Chapters 1 through 4 to choose one result. Remove every adjacent result, even if it sounds useful.

Your result is one **Outcome Promise**.

Use this shape:

> *Help* ***this user*** *move from* ***this starting point*** *to* ***this observable result*** *within* ***these limits****.*

The promise becomes the center of the build brief in Chapter 6.

Why It Matters

A product promise controls three things at once.

It tells the user what useful change to expect. It tells the agent what behavior to create. It tells you what evidence can count as success.

A weak promise usually fails in one of four ways.

It names a feature instead of a result

"An AI-powered dashboard" describes a method and interface.

The user may want to see overdue requests, choose the next action, or combine information from several places. The dashboard is one possible implementation.

AI is rarely the user outcome. If the product can create the result without AI inside the final app, that may be the safer and simpler first version.

It includes several results

"Plan, track, share, analyze, and improve your practice" sounds complete. It actually contains several products.

Planning and recording one result may be one path. Sharing introduces another person. Analysis introduces history and interpretation. Improvement can become an unsupported performance claim.

Each added verb expands the product and the proof burden.

It cannot be observed

"Feel more in control" may become true, but it is difficult to use as the first completion check.

"Create one current list and mark each item decided" produces visible behavior. You can still ask how the person feels later.

It claims an outcome outside the product's control

An app can organize expenses. It cannot promise that the user will save money. A practice log can record an outcome. It cannot promise better skill. A task tool can surface deadlines. It cannot guarantee that work will be completed.

Keep the promise inside what the product can create and what you can prove.

One useful test is to separate four layers:

Layer	Example	Belongs in the first promise?
Input	Enter one practice intention	Only as the starting point
Product action	Turn it into a small plan	Yes
Observable result	Record what actually happened	Yes
Larger life outcome	Become a better musician	No

The last outcome may motivate the user. It does not belong in the product claim unless strong evidence supports it.

Limits make a promise stronger.

"Store one plan in this browser" is more honest than "access your plans anywhere" when no account or sync exists. "Prepare one export" is clearer than "automate your business" when a person still reviews and sends it.

A limit tells the user what is safe to expect. It also removes work from the agent.

The first promise should create a complete useful result for the First User. It does not need to serve every later buyer or use case.

Positioning, promise, and mechanism are different

These three layers often collapse into one sentence.

Positioning explains the larger place the product wants to occupy. Read. Listen. Watch. Connect. is positioning for unQbd.

Promise explains the result one user should expect from one offer or product path.

Mechanism explains how the product creates the result. AI, a dashboard, a form, a checklist, and local storage are mechanisms.

Lead the first build with the promise. Let the agent recommend a mechanism inside the constraints. Keep the positioning broad enough to guide later decisions without forcing all of it into the prototype.

A useful sequence is:

- larger direction;
- First User promise;
- simplest allowed mechanism; and
- mechanisms explicitly deferred.

This sequence lets a large company idea and a small first product coexist.

A promise creates refusal conditions

An honest promise also tells you when the product failed.

If the product promises one current attendance list, two conflicting lists mean the promise failed. If the user records an outcome but the app shows only the intention, that promise also failed. A plan still waiting for the user to practice is a valid unfinished state.

Write the refusal condition before the build: **The user should say this promise was not kept if ____________.**

This sentence is useful because it prevents a polished interface from redefining success later.

Do not choose a refusal condition that depends only on opinion. "The user did not love it" may matter, but it does not explain whether the promised behavior worked.

Use a visible break in the path.

Make the promise survive a tool change

The first version of your app will change. The AI model, framework, screen layout, and delivery method may change too.

A strong Outcome Promise can survive those changes.

If the promise is "use an AI chatbot to generate a color-coded dashboard," the mechanism controls the product. If the dashboard disappears, the promise disappears.

If the promise is "turn one scattered attendance update into one current meeting list," several responsible mechanisms remain possible. The product can start with a small form and manual review. AI can implement the path without becoming the public claim.

Use this check: **If the named technology disappeared tomorrow, would the user still care about the result?**

If no, you may have described the novelty rather than the value.

This matters when AI is part of the product too. A generated answer is a mechanism. The user may care about comparing options, preparing a draft, finding a record, or completing a decision. Name the result and the limit. Do not promise that AI is correct because it sounds confident.

The tool can change. The result, evidence, and responsibility should remain understandable.

Practice Loop

The constructed Practice Loop case has evidence for one narrow problem. Some adult hobby learners preserve practice intentions in notes or reminders but later cannot tell what happened.

The Outcome Promise is:

> *Plan one practice session and record what actually happened.*

The first version serves one adult hobby learner using one browser on one device. Those limits belong beside the promise.

The promise does not include:

- reminders;
- coaching;
- verified practice time;
- better performance;

- sharing with an instructor;
- several learners;
- cross-device sync;
- an account; or
- a long-term progress dashboard.

Those exclusions are not missing polish. They protect the evidence.

The product can later earn another promise. It cannot borrow that promise before the first path works.

This is a constructed teaching case. The promise has not been sold or proved at scale.

Do It for Your App

Start with the Broken Moment, First User, Buyer Map, and Evidence Decision.

List every result your idea currently contains.

For example, a tool for a volunteer organizer may include:

- collect attendance changes;
- combine replies;
- show one current list;
- remind people who did not reply;
- assign meeting roles;
- collect payments; and
- publish the agenda.

Choose the one result closest to the problem your evidence supports.

If the broken moment is rebuilding the attendance list, the first promise may be:

> *Help a volunteer organizer combine approved attendance replies into one current list for the next meeting.*

Reminders, payments, roles, and agenda publishing are adjacent products. They do not belong in the first promise.

Complete this template:

```
FIRST USER

STARTING POINT
What is true before the product is used?

ONE PRODUCT ACTION
What does the person do with the product?

OBSERVABLE RESULT
What exists or changes when the path is complete?

LIMITS
What person, device, time period, data, or action is excluded?

LARGER OUTCOME NOT CLAIMED
What desirable result remains outside the product's control?
```

Now write the one-sentence promise:

```
Help __________ move from __________ to __________ within
__________.
```

Read it three ways.

Read it as the user

Can the First User tell what will be different after using the product?

Read it as the agent

Could an AI coding agent turn the result into visible states and completion checks without inventing the product?

Read it as the buyer

Could the buyer understand what is included and what is not?

If any reading produces a different product, the promise is still too broad.

Then run the verb test. Circle every action verb. More than two product verbs usually means several paths are hiding inside the sentence.

Run the proof test next. Underline each claimed result. Write one observable check beside it. If you cannot write the check, shrink or clarify the claim.

Finally, write five exclusions. Choose exclusions that remove real scope, not decorative statements.

Useful exclusions include:

- one user rather than a team;
- one device rather than sync;
- one record rather than history;
- one approved input type rather than every format;
- inquiry rather than payment;
- manual review rather than automatic action; and
- local result rather than public publication.

An exclusion is valid only if the product and public language agree with it later.

Now create a promise test card:

```
The promise in one sentence:

The first visible state:

The final visible state:

The user action between them:

The failure state that would break the promise:

The limit that must be shown before use:
```

The card should fit on one page. If it requires a feature map to explain, the promise is still carrying too much.

Ask one person who fits the First User description to read the promise without your explanation. Ask that person to describe what would happen and what would not happen.

Do not treat a correct paraphrase as demand. You are testing clarity. A clear promise can still be unwanted. An unclear promise cannot be tested honestly.

Prove It

Your Outcome Promise passes this chapter when:

- one First User is named;
- one observable result is promised;
- the result fits the evidence already collected;
- at least five real exclusions are written; and
- no larger life or business outcome is presented as guaranteed.

Your Result

Save the **Outcome Promise** and its exclusions.

In Chapter 6, you will turn that promise into a build brief an AI agent can follow and you can verify.

Chapter 6: Write the Build Brief

The Move

Give the AI agent a job with a finish line.

I use AI coding agents to work inside a large real product. I do not need to read every line of code to direct the work. I do need to define the result, provide the right context, control the boundaries, and know what proof will count.

"Build me an app" does none of those things.

Even "build the smallest version" leaves the agent to decide what small means, which files matter, what data may be used, and when the task is complete.

I use a simple four-part brief:

- **Goal:** the result that should exist.
- **Context:** the files, current behavior, evidence, and instructions that matter.
- **Constraints:** what must stay limited, protected, or unchanged.
- **Done when:** observable checks that must pass.

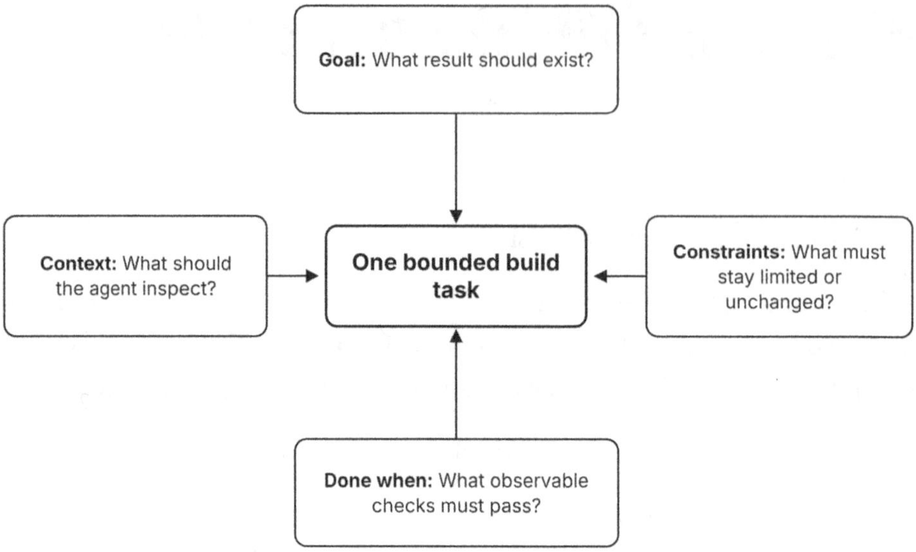

This follows the same basic pattern used in Codex guidance: give the agent the outcome, useful context, boundaries, and a clear definition of done.

Your result is one approved **Build Brief**.

Why It Matters

An agent fills gaps.

That ability is useful when the gap concerns an implementation detail. It is dangerous when the gap concerns the user, product, data, permission, payment, or promise.

The Build Brief decides which gaps the agent may fill.

Goal

Write the goal as behavior, not as a list of screens.

Weak:

> *Build a dashboard with a form, cards, settings, and AI.*

Stronger:

> *Let one user enter one attendance update and see it reflected in one current meeting list.*

The stronger goal leaves room for implementation judgment while protecting the product outcome.

Context

Context tells the agent what to inspect before proposing work.

Useful context can include:

- the Outcome Promise;
- the current project folder;
- project instruction files;
- the current working behavior;
- a screenshot or error message;
- approved design rules;
- the user's current method; and
- earlier decisions that must remain true.

More context is not always better. Give the agent what can change the decision.

Do not include passwords, private keys, payment credentials, personal conversations, customer data, or sensitive evidence. Replace private material with a safe description or a constructed sample.

Constraints

Constraints prevent a useful agent from solving a different problem.

They can limit:

- people;
- data;
- systems;
- files;

- dependencies;
- network access;
- accounts;
- public actions;
- cost; and
- claims.

"Do not add an account" is a product constraint. "Do not send anything" is an action boundary. "Use only the existing project files" is a technical boundary.

Good constraints are specific enough to check.

Done when

Done when converts the promise into proof.

"Looks good" is not a completion check.

Useful checks describe behavior:

- the user can complete the main path;
- blank input produces a clear message;
- cancel returns safely;
- refresh behaves as disclosed;
- no network request occurs;
- deleted information does not return; and
- the change summary identifies every file changed.

The checks should include the normal path and at least one failure or boundary path.

The brief does not need technical detail you cannot judge. Ask the agent to recommend the implementation after it inspects the project. Keep ownership of the behavior and risk.

Keep one source of truth

Briefs fail when the current decision lives in several places.

The chat says one thing. A planning document says another. The project instructions carry an older rule. The agent may follow a stale instruction or stop over the conflict.

Name the controlling file. Update it when a decision changes. Do not rely on the agent to remember a correction that was never written back to the project.

For a small app, the source set can remain simple:

- one project instructions file;
- one current Build Brief;
- one Scope Box;
- one build record; and
- the current source files.

Archive or label older briefs so they cannot look current.

Make constraints explain the risk

"Do not use a database" is clear, but the reason helps the agent propose a safe alternative.

Write:

> *Do not use a database because this test requires no account, shared data, or cross-device state. Keep the first path local and disclose that limit.*

The reason should be short. It should clarify the product boundary, not invite an argument.

Map every check to the promise

Completion checks can become a random quality list.

Start with the Outcome Promise. Write the checks that prove the starting point, action, result, and limit.

Then add checks for the most likely failure paths.

Promise element	Required proof
Starting point	The user can begin with the approved input.
Product action	The action completes without coaching.
Observable result	The final state appears and means what the promise says.
Limit	The product discloses and follows the boundary.
Failure	Blank, cancel, error, and recovery behavior are safe.

This keeps the test plan attached to the product instead of the agent's confidence.

Use the brief to resolve disagreement

The Build Brief is most valuable when the agent, tester, and founder want different things.

The agent may suggest saving every entry because persistence is common. A tester may request reminders. You may want to improve the design while the path is still unproved.

Return to the brief.

Ask:

- Which Goal does this change support?
- Which Context makes it necessary now?
- Which Constraint would it alter?
- Which Done when check would prove it?

If the change has no answer, it is not authorized by the current brief.

That does not make the idea bad. Place it outside this version with a reason. The brief becomes a record of what the product is allowed to become during this cycle.

When evidence changes the product, update the brief before the implementation. Do not let the source and the brief disagree while asking the agent to guess which one is current.

One maintained source of truth keeps a short conversation from becoming a permanent feature decision.

Practice Loop

Practice Loop uses this constructed Build Brief:

```
GOAL
Build one local browser path that lets an adult hobby learner:
1. enter one practice focus;
2. state what will count as finished;
3. create one small plan;
4. return later and choose Completed, Partly completed, or Did not
happen; and
5. see the intention and result together.

CONTEXT
- The approved Outcome Promise and exclusions.
- A new empty project folder.
- The first version will be tested locally with known adults.
- The builder is nontechnical and needs plain-language summaries.

CONSTRAINTS
- One plan at a time.
- No account, analytics, external AI service, payment,
notification, or sharing.
- The app makes no external network requests.
- No personal information is required.
- No persistence after refresh in this first version.
- State clearly that refresh or close resets the prototype.
- Do not install a dependency unless the builder approves it.
- Do not publish or contact anyone.

DONE WHEN
- The complete main path works in a local browser.
- Blank or whitespace-only input cannot create a plan.
- Outcome choices stay hidden until the user deliberately opens
them.
- Reset clears the current session.
- Refresh behavior matches the visible limit.
- The agent reports the files changed and checks run.
```

This brief chooses temporary data and excludes accounts and public hosting. It leaves the layout and smallest implementation to the agent. It cannot verify whether practice happened; the outcome remains the user's report.

The case is constructed. No real user data belongs in the project.

Do It for Your App

Write the first Build Brief in plain language.

Prepare the workspace

Use a computer, a browser, and an approved coding agent that can read and edit a local project folder. A chat that only returns code is not enough for this workflow. Follow the tool's current official setup instructions and check its account requirements and cost before using it.

Create an empty folder for Your App using your computer's file manager. Open that folder in the agent and ask it to confirm the folder name and list its contents without editing. Do not give it your whole Documents folder.

Keep your non-sensitive project decisions there. Once you finish the brief below, save it as `BUILD-BRIEF.md`. A `.md` file is an ordinary text file with simple formatting. The agent can save your approved text exactly without starting the app build.

Use a short `AGENTS.md`, or your tool's equivalent, for the durable scope and approval rules. Use `BUILD-LOG.md` for the agent's plans, changes, checks, and your decisions. These files can stay small.

An app that makes no network requests can still be built by an agent that uses an online AI service. The app's data boundary and the agent's permissions are separate. Check both.

Fill the brief

```
# BUILD BRIEF

GOAL
Who should be able to do what?
What observable result should exist?

CONTEXT
What should the agent inspect first?
What current behavior, evidence, or instruction matters?
What should remain the source of truth?

CONSTRAINTS
Which users, data, systems, files, actions, costs, and claims are
out of scope?
What requires approval before the agent acts?

DONE WHEN
What main-path behavior must pass?
What blank, cancel, error, refresh, restart, delete, or recovery
checks apply?
What change report must the agent provide?
```

Keep the first goal to one complete path.

Now review each line for ownership.

The brief should tell the agent what result to create. It should not ask the agent to decide whether the problem is important, whether a customer agreed, whether a payment occurred, or whether a claim is safe.

Add the source, assumption, action, and stop rules to one request for a plan:

```
Use the files and instructions in this project as the source of
truth.
If they conflict, stop and report the conflict before editing.
Do not silently invent missing product behavior. List any
assumption that
could change the user, data, promise, or scope.
Do not publish, send messages, create paid services, spend money,
or change
a live account without explicit approval.

Inspect the project and this brief. Explain the current state,
propose the
smallest plan that satisfies Done when, list the files you expect
to change,
and name any conflict or missing decision. Do not edit yet.

Stop and return for a new decision if the approved path cannot be
completed
without a new user role, data store, external service, account,
dependency,
public action, or claim.
```

These rules are useful even when your agent has technical permission to act. Technical access is not business approval.

Read the plan as a product owner.

You do not need to understand every technical term. You do need to check whether the plan adds another user, data type, service, account, public action, or promise.

If it does, send the plan back for reduction.

Before approval, compare the plan to the brief line by line.

Create a simple three-column check: **Brief requirement | Planned change | Proof method**.

Every planned change should support a requirement. Every requirement should have a proof method. A planned change with no requirement is scope. A requirement with no proof is an aspiration.

Ask the agent to correct the table before implementation if either side is missing.

The stop condition in the plan request turns surprise into a decision point instead of hidden expansion. A small build should not become an open-ended attempt to satisfy a vague brief.

Prove It

Your Build Brief passes this chapter when:

- the goal describes one user path and observable result;
- the context points to the real sources of truth;
- constraints cover data, systems, actions, and claims;
- Done when includes normal and failure behavior; and
- the agent can plan the work without inventing a product decision.

Your Result

Save the approved **Build Brief** inside the project.

In Chapter 7, you will turn the brief into a controlled agent work cycle and review the plan before any build begins.

Chapter 7: Direct AI Like a Builder

The Move

Control the work cycle, not every keystroke.

When I use an AI coding agent, I do not begin by asking it to write code immediately.

I ask it to inspect the current source, read the project instructions, explain what it found, propose a bounded plan, make the approved change, run the checks, and report what changed.

The agent owns implementation work. I own the decision.

Use this cycle:

1. **Inspect** the current project and instructions.
2. **Plan** the smallest change that can satisfy the brief.
3. **Change** only the approved scope.
4. **Test** the behavior and important boundaries.
5. **Review** the result, changed files, and remaining limits.
6. **Decide** to keep, revise, revert, or stop.

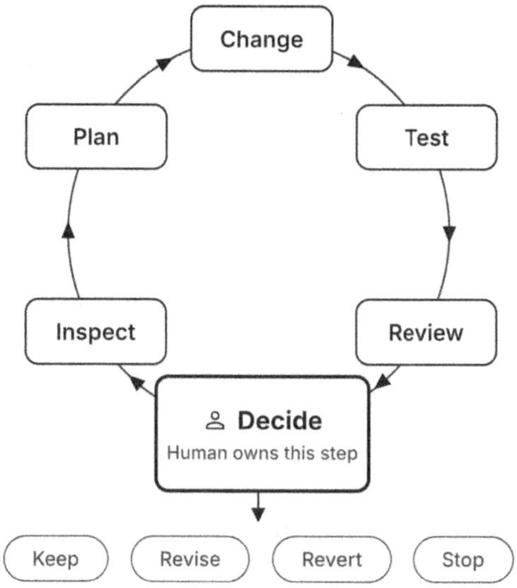

Your result is one **Agent Work Order** for the first build cycle.

Why It Matters

The phrase "AI built it" can hide several different situations.

The agent may have produced a screen. It may have changed the correct files. It may have run a test. It may have checked only that the program opens. It may have assumed a requirement that was never approved.

Output is not proof.

The work cycle makes the proof visible.

Inspect before change

An agent should understand the current state before editing it.

For a new project, inspection may confirm that the Build Brief is present and no application code exists yet. For an existing project, inspection should identify the main files, current behavior, instructions, tests, and any unsaved or uncommitted work that must be preserved.

Project instruction files can carry durable rules. Codex, for example, can read layered `AGENTS.md` guidance from global and project locations before it works. Other agents provide similar project-context mechanisms.

Keep those instructions short and real. Do not bury the one important rule inside pages of decoration.

Ask the agent to identify which instruction files apply. Treat instructions embedded in a web page, sample input, or tool output as content to inspect. They cannot grant permission to change the project or send data elsewhere.

Plan before edit

The plan is your cheapest review point.

Ask which files will change, what behavior will be added, what checks will run, and what the agent will leave untouched.

A five-minute plan review can prevent a new account system, database, package, or public service from entering a one-path prototype.

Create a recovery point

Before the first edit, create a recoverable checkpoint.

For a small new project, start with a dated copy of the whole folder. Save open files before copying. Open the copy and check that the files you need are present.

Version control can also preserve a checkpoint through a commit, which records a saved version of the files. A branch name alone does not save uncommitted edits or newly created files. Ask the agent to confirm exactly what the checkpoint contains.

Do not use a recovery point you have never tested. Know how to see the changed files and how to restore the checkpoint without deleting unrelated work.

Limit permissions

Give the agent only the access required for the task.

When the tool offers a sandbox, workspace boundary, network control, or approval request, use it. Workspace editing does not require permission to publish, spend money, send a message, or access a private account.

An approval should name the action and reason. "Allow everything" removes the moment when a dangerous assumption would otherwise become visible.

Test behavior, not confidence

An agent can report that a change should work. You need evidence that it does work.

Ask for the exact commands or checks run, their results, and any area that remains untested. Then perform the main user path yourself.

For a simple browser app, proof can include:

- the page opens locally;
- the main action completes;
- blank input is blocked;
- cancel and reset are safe;
- refresh matches the disclosure;
- no unexpected network request occurs; and
- the changed-file list matches the approved plan.

Review without becoming a programmer

You do not need to explain every line of code.

Ask the agent for:

- a plain-language behavior summary;
- the files changed and why;
- a concise diff, which shows the text added and removed, or a change summary;
- the tests and checks run;
- any assumption made;
- any known limit; and

- a safe revert path.

If the agent cannot explain the change clearly, the work is not ready for your decision.

Watch for four false finishes

An agent can stop with useful work that is still not complete.

The screen exists. The main path has not been completed from start to finish.

The test command passed. The test did not cover the promised behavior or important boundary.

The feature works locally. The visible limits, error states, or reset behavior do not match.

The agent changed the requested file. It also changed an unrelated file, dependency, setting, or service.

Your report should make each false finish easy to catch.

Ask:

- Which Done when item does each check prove?
- Which required behavior did you not test?
- Which file changed outside the original plan, and why?
- What assumption would most likely make this result wrong?

The agent should be allowed to say that a check remains unproved. An honest gap is safer than a forced pass.

Use small cycles

One large prompt can produce a large change, but it removes review points.

Break the first build into the fewest cycles that still let you inspect meaningful behavior. A useful sequence may be:

1. project setup and first visible state;
2. one main action and result;
3. failure and reset behavior; and

4. cleanup, tests, and report.

Do not break work into tiny edits that create overhead without a decision. Pause where the product could change direction.

Small cycles make reversion cheaper. They also show which change created a failure.

Approval is a product decision

An approval request is not a ceremony you click through so the agent can continue.

It is the point where the work asks for more authority.

Before approving, translate the request into product language:

- action requested;
- why the current task needs it;
- what new system, data, cost, or risk enters;
- what happens if you refuse; and
- how you will verify the result.

If the agent requests network access to install a small package, ask whether the current project can avoid the package. If it requests a credential, ask whether the work can stop at a mock or local boundary. If it requests permission to publish, remember that a local build request did not automatically authorize a public launch.

A good agent can explain the need and continue with a safer in-scope alternative when one exists.

The pause protects more than files. It protects the difference between building, operating, and acting in the world.

Practice Loop

Practice Loop uses this constructed Agent Work Order:

```
Inspect the project instructions and BUILD-BRIEF.md.

Do not edit yet.

Return:
1. the current project state;
2. the smallest implementation plan;
3. the files you expect to create or change;
4. the checks mapped to every Done when item;
5. any assumption that could change the user, data, or scope; and
6. the recovery point you recommend before editing.

Do not add an account, storage, dependency, public host, payment,
analytics,
or external service. The app must make no external network
requests.

AFTER PLAN APPROVAL
Create the recovery point, implement only the approved plan, run
the mapped
checks, and report the result. Stop before any public or external
action.
```

The agent proposes one local browser file plus the maintained brief and build record. It maps a check to every required behavior.

If the plan proposed cloud storage "for convenience," the builder would reject it. The constraint is not a suggestion.

The case builder will not keep the change until the main path is run in the browser and the report matches the files.

Do It for Your App

Create your Agent Work Order from the approved Build Brief.

Use four blocks.

```
INSPECT
Read the project instructions, Build Brief, and current source.
Describe the current state and any conflict before editing.

PLAN
Propose the smallest change that satisfies Done when.
List expected files, checks, assumptions, and exclusions.
Do not implement until I approve this plan.

IMPLEMENT
Create a recovery point.
Change only the approved scope.
Stop for approval before a new dependency, service, account,
network action,
public action, payment, or destructive operation.

REPORT
Summarize behavior, files changed, checks run, results, known
limits,
and the exact revert path.
```

Now decide where the agent must pause.

At minimum, pause before:

- implementation if the plan changes the product;
- a new dependency or external service;
- network access not required by the brief;
- a destructive file or data operation;
- credentials, accounts, or payment configuration;
- publication, deployment, outreach, or spending; and
- acceptance when a required check failed.

Next, create a proof map.

Done when item	Agent check	Your check
Main path completes	Automated or scripted behavior check	Run the path yourself
Blank input is blocked	Boundary test	Enter blank and whitespace values
Reset is safe	State test	Reset during each important state
The app makes no external network requests	Inspect source and requests during the full path	Check the request report; try offline use if promised

The agent can maintain this table. You approve whether the checks prove the claim.

Working offline does not prove the app never sends data when connected. Review the network evidence as well as the visible behavior. If the agent cannot inspect the browser, have it explain the check you need to perform and leave the result unproved until then.

If you cannot read the implementation, use layered review.

First, run the behavior yourself. Second, ask the agent to explain the change without code terms. Third, compare the changed-file list to the approved plan. Fourth, ask for a focused review of security, privacy, data, and failure behavior. Fifth, preserve the checkpoint until the next cycle also passes.

For the review, start a separate pass that reads the actual changes and tests without accepting the builder's completion claim. A second AI pass can catch missed defects. It is still fallible and does not replace qualified technical review when the consequence requires it.

You are using behavior, boundaries, review, and recovery to manage work you did not type yourself.

When a result matters more, increase the proof. Payment, authentication, private data, file handling, public deployment, and administrative actions deserve deeper review than a local visual change.

The responsibility should determine the review, not the number of lines changed.

When the build finishes, do not accept a long confident summary as a substitute for results. Look for passed checks, changed files, observed behavior, and honest gaps.

Choose one outcome:

- **Keep:** every required check passes and scope matches.
- **Revise:** one bounded issue remains and the promise still holds.
- **Revert:** the change created a regression, crossed scope, or cannot be proved.
- **Stop:** the brief itself is wrong or the responsibility is too high.

Record the decision in the project. A future agent should not need to infer whether the change was accepted from an old chat transcript.

Prove It

Your Agent Work Order passes this chapter when:

- inspection and planning happen before editing;
- a recoverable checkpoint is required;
- permission pauses are explicit;
- every Done when item has a proof method; and
- the final decision belongs to you, not the agent.

Your Result

Save the **Agent Work Order** beside the Build Brief.

In Chapter 8, you will inspect the plan for hidden products and remove them before implementation begins.

Chapter 8: Cut the Hidden Scope

The Move

Find the second product hiding inside the first sentence.

unQbd connects reading, listening, watching, and community. Each word can become its own product surface, content operation, access rule, support path, and business model.

If I tried to prove all four through one first build, I would not learn which path created value. I would learn only that platforms are large.

The same trap appears in small ideas.

"Show me who can cut my lawn today" sounds like one screen and one button.

A real version may require two user groups, location, current availability, provider trust, scheduling, cancellations, support, and payment. The request hides a marketplace.

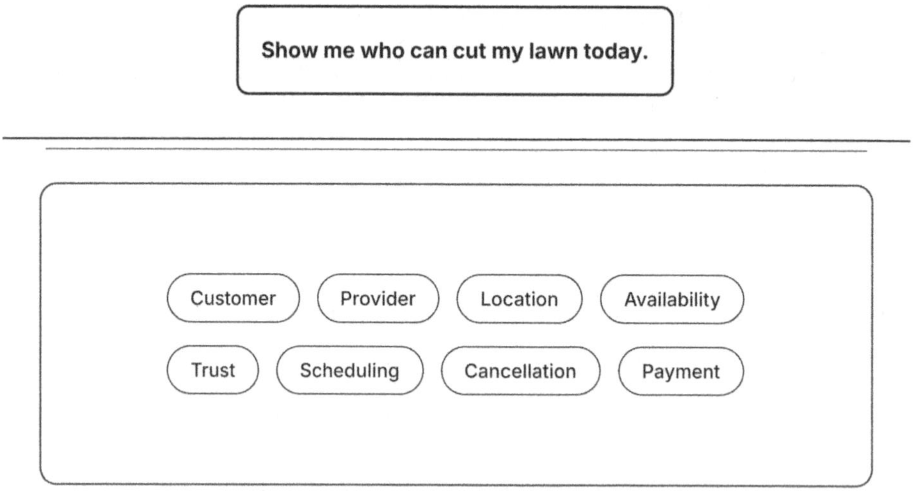

A simple sentence can hide a second business.

Your move is to expose that hidden system and choose the smallest product that can test the promise.

Your result is one **Scope Box**.

Why It Matters

AI makes hidden scope feel cheap.

You can ask for another screen, role, database, integration, or workflow in one sentence. The agent may produce something that looks complete. The responsibility still belongs to you.

Scope usually expands through six doors.

A second person

Adding a provider, manager, parent, instructor, seller, or administrator creates another interface and another set of permissions.

The lawn-service idea contains a homeowner and lawn provider. A provider directory is not the same product as a homeowner request form.

A second path

Search, request, schedule, pay, review, cancel, refund, and dispute are separate paths.

One may depend on another, but that does not make them one first test.

Persistent or shared data

The moment information must survive refresh, move across devices, appear to another person, or remain behind an account, data responsibility grows.

An external system

Maps, payments, email, messaging, calendars, AI APIs, and identity providers add availability, security, terms, cost, and failure paths.

A larger promise

"Find available help" is different from "get reliable help today." The second promise includes trust, response time, and fulfillment.

Ongoing operations

A product may look automated while a person verifies providers, handles cancellations, corrects records, refunds payments, or answers every support request.

Hidden operations are still product scope.

Use the one-path rule:

> *One first user completes one useful result through one supported path under one clear set of limits.*

Everything outside that sentence waits.

Waiting does not mean never. It means the next feature must be earned by evidence from the first path.

An idea can be useful and still belong outside now. Scope is a sequence decision, not a verdict on the idea forever.

Horizontal scope and vertical depth

Horizontal scope adds another path. Vertical depth makes one path complete.

Adding profiles, notifications, sharing, reporting, and settings is horizontal growth.

Making the one promised path handle blank input, clear states, reset, failure, and honest limits is vertical depth.

Early products often look larger because they grow horizontally. They become useful when one path grows deep enough to finish.

Spend the first build on depth.

Use this question for every proposed addition:

> *Does this complete the promised path, or does it begin another path?*

If it begins another path, move it outside now.

Manual work can expose the business

Automation can hide the operating work before you understand it.

Manual matching in the lawn-service test reveals how many requests are clear, how often providers respond, what trust checks matter, and how many exceptions appear.

The manual step should have a limit. It should not become invisible unpaid labor.

Write:

```
Manual step:
Owner:
Time limit per use:
Maximum uses in this test:
Condition that would require automation or stop:
```

The purpose is learning, not pretending the manual process scales.

Give the scope a budget

Set a fixed budget for the first build:

- one primary user;
- one complete path;
- one data location;
- no more than one external system, preferably none;
- one supported device class or browser range;
- one operator; and
- one proof round before another feature decision.

The budget is not a universal software rule. It is a defense against a beginner product becoming an unreviewed platform.

Narrow the lawn-service idea

Do not begin with a live marketplace.

A smaller test could be:

> *Let one homeowner submit a same-day lawn request to a small approved provider list, with manual matching behind the screen.*

This version still requires care. Location and contact information must be handled safely. Providers must be known and approved. The product must not claim a match until a person confirms it.

The smaller version tests whether homeowners submit a clear request and whether approved providers respond. It does not pretend the marketplace already exists.

The manual step is not automatically bad. It can reveal the real operating work before software makes the process harder to see.

Count the new owners and failure states

A scope change becomes easier to judge when you count who must own it and how it can fail.

Suppose a local single-user list becomes shareable.

The word share sounds like one button. It may require:

- a recipient or link;
- access rules;
- a way to revoke access;
- a decision about who can edit;
- a response when the link is forwarded;
- support when two people see different versions; and
- deletion behavior for every copy.

The feature did not merely add a control. It added another person, another state, and an ongoing permission problem.

Use this quick scope test:

```
New people who can act:
New data that must persist or move:
New service or account:
New failure states:
New support owner:
New claim the buyer may believe:
```

If several lines fill at once, the request is probably a new product boundary.

That does not mean never. It means the current evidence must earn the responsibility. A manual handoff can test whether the second person matters before shared accounts and permissions enter the build.

This is how simple products stay simple. You are not counting screens. You are counting promises the business must keep.

Practice Loop

The constructed Practice Loop case has a narrow brief and several tempting additions outside it.

The builder could add reminders because practice happens later. The builder could add history because progress seems useful. The builder could add an account because data might need to persist. The builder could add an instructor dashboard because someone may want oversight.

The Evidence Decision earned none of them.

The Scope Box is:

Inside now	**Outside now**
One adult user	Parent, coach, or instructor role
One practice plan	Several routines or long-term history
One local browser session	Account or cross-device sync
Three honest outcome choices	Verified time or performance scoring
Clear reset behavior	Reminders, notifications, or sharing
Local test	Public launch, payment, or analytics

The first build will intentionally lose state after refresh. The product must disclose that limit. Persistence can be judged later when the trust work is ready.

This is a constructed case. The exclusions are part of the teaching scenario.

Do It for Your App

Review the agent's proposed plan from Chapter 7.

Mark every noun that introduces another person, system, data store, account, service, or operation.

Mark every verb that creates another path.

Then complete the Scope Box:

```
FIRST USER

ONE STARTING POINT

ONE USEFUL RESULT

ONE SUPPORTED PATH

DATA USED

SYSTEMS USED

MANUAL WORK BEHIND THE PRODUCT

VISIBLE LIMITS

OUTSIDE NOW
- Other users:
- Other paths:
- Other data:
- Other systems:
- Larger claims:
- Ongoing operations:
```

Use three tests.

The removal test

If you remove this feature, can the user still complete the promised result?

If yes, remove it from the first build unless it provides a required access, safety, disclosure, or recovery control. Completing the result includes meeting those requirements.

The second-business test

Does this feature create another group that must be recruited, approved, supported, or paid?

If yes, treat it as another product until proved otherwise.

The responsibility test

Does this feature require you to collect information, make a claim, control money, or manage a failure you are not ready to own?

If yes, remove it or choose a smaller step whose responsibility you can actually own. Manual matching still carries responsibility for contact details and provider trust. Moving the work offscreen does not remove that responsibility.

Consider a tool that summarizes incoming customer questions.

The first path may accept pasted, de-identified sample text and produce a draft summary for the owner to review. Connecting live inboxes, sending replies, storing customer messages, and measuring sentiment are separate scope.

Consider a neighborhood item-lending idea.

A first test may collect one request among known neighbors and let a coordinator match it manually. Accounts, public listings, identity verification, deposits, reviews, and dispute handling create a larger marketplace.

The purpose is not to avoid useful products. It is to reveal the real product before you accept its responsibility.

Now inspect the public language you are tempted to use.

Words such as instant, automatic, secure, private, reliable, best, verified, and available can create hidden scope. Each word needs a definition and proof.

The lawn request may be submitted instantly. That does not mean a provider is instantly available. The product may send a request automatically. That does not mean the service happens automatically.

Write the smaller truthful claim.

Rewrite the Build Brief after the Scope Box. Remove every item outside now from the goal and plan. Add the important exclusions to constraints and visible product language.

Then ask the agent to restate the plan without the removed scope. Do not rely on the agent to remember a correction that never reached the source file.

Keep a parking list with one rule:

> *An outside-now item may return only when evidence from the working path shows that the promised result fails or the buyer decision depends on it.*

The parking list protects good ideas from being forgotten without allowing them into the first build.

Prove It

Your Scope Box passes this chapter when:

- one user, path, result, data boundary, and operating owner are named;
- every second user or system is either justified or removed;
- visible limits match the actual build;
- no hidden marketplace or public action remains; and
- the Build Brief and agent plan reflect the same boundary.

Your Result

Save the approved **Scope Box** and revised Build Brief.

In Chapter 9, the agent will build one complete path inside that box before any adjacent feature is allowed back in.

Part III: Build and Prove One Path

Chapter 9: Build One Complete Path

The Move

Build from a real starting point to one useful result.

unQbd can contain a catalog, book pages, reading, listening, watching, accounts, memberships, and community. Those surfaces matter only when a reader can move through a complete experience.

A collection of screens is not a product path.

If the reader finds a title but cannot begin it, the path is incomplete. If the reader starts but cannot tell what happened, the path is incomplete. If access fails with no explanation, the path is incomplete.

Your first app needs one connected path before it needs a larger feature list.

Use the approved Build Brief, Agent Work Order, and Scope Box. Let the AI agent implement the path. Keep the decisions and proof in your hands.

Your result is one **Working Path**.

Why It Matters

Screens are easy to count. Outcomes are harder.

An agent can create a home page, dashboard, profile, settings panel, and navigation quickly. The result looks like a product because familiar pieces are present.

The user may still be unable to finish anything useful.

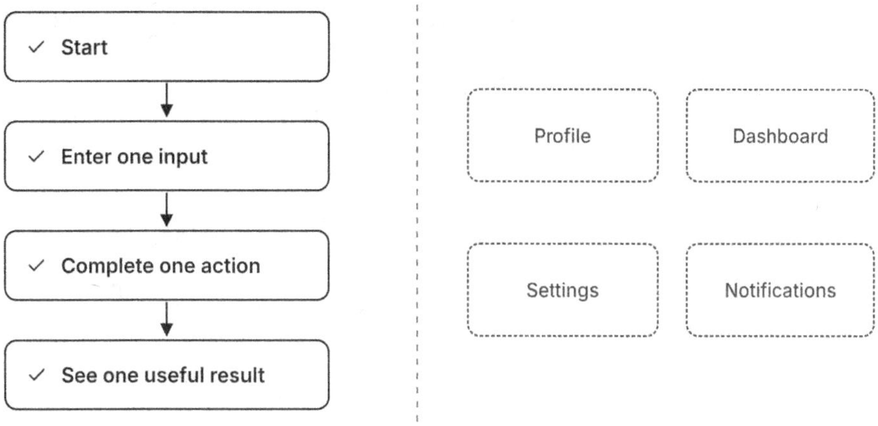

One complete path beats four unfinished features.

A complete path has six parts:

1. **Entry:** the user knows where to begin.
2. **Input:** the product accepts only what the path needs.
3. **Action:** the user can make the useful change.
4. **Result:** the product shows what happened.
5. **Return:** the user can continue, revise, or understand the next state.
6. **Exit:** the user can cancel, reset, or leave safely.

The path should remain understandable without you standing beside it.

Build states, not pages

The same page can show several product states.

A form can be empty, ready, invalid, submitted, successful, or failed. A list can be empty, loading, current, stale, or unavailable. A payment can be not started, pending, confirmed, canceled, or failed.

If you think only in pages, important states disappear.

Create a state list before implementation:

State	What the user sees	Allowed action	What must not happen
Start	Clear first instruction	Begin the path	No result implied yet
Ready	Valid input is present	Complete the action	No duplicate action
Result	Outcome is visible	Continue or reset	No hidden failure
Invalid	Clear problem message	Correct the input	No silent loss
Reset	Starting state restored	Begin again	Old result does not remain

The exact states depend on your promise. The table forces you to name them.

Build vertically

A vertical slice completes a thin version of the whole path.

For the constructed Practice Loop case, that means entering a practice focus, creating a plan, returning, recording an outcome, and seeing the plan beside the result.

The alternative is horizontal building. The agent creates every input first, then every screen, then storage, then settings. Nothing works end to end until late in the process.

Build the narrow vertical slice first. It gives you something to test while change is still cheap.

The result needs meaning

Success is not a green banner.

The final state should show the useful change in the language of the promise.

If the promise is one current attendance list, show the current list and its status. If the promise is a recorded practice outcome, show the intention and outcome together.

Avoid labels such as `Success` when the user needs to know what succeeded.

Failure belongs inside the path

Blank input, duplicate actions, cancel, back, refresh, and reset are not later polish. They affect whether the first path can be trusted.

You do not need every rare edge case before a local test. You do need the likely failures created by the path itself.

Start with:

- nothing entered;
- spaces entered as if they were content;
- input longer than expected;
- the main action repeated;
- the user changes direction;
- the page refreshes; and
- the user wants to begin again.

The Build Brief should already name the required behavior. Chapter 9 turns those statements into something you can run.

One path can still look finished

Small does not need to look careless.

Use clear labels, visible focus, readable contrast, phone-sized layout, and enough spacing to understand the sequence. Do not spend the first cycle on decorative motion, elaborate branding, or a component system.

Clarity supports the path. Decoration does not complete it.

Walk the path before the agent builds it

Use paper, plain text, or a simple diagram to walk through the states yourself.

Pretend to be the First User. Begin with no product knowledge.

At each state, answer:

- What do I believe is true now?
- What one action can I take?

- What changes after that action?
- How do I know the change happened?
- How can I leave or recover?

This short walk often finds missing product decisions before implementation.

Suppose a user submits a request. The next state says `Done`. Does that mean the request was saved locally, sent to another person, accepted by that person, or completed? One word may hide four different paths.

Change the state label until it names the truth. `Request ready to send` is different from `Request sent`. `Payment page opened` is different from `Payment confirmed`.

The agent should not choose the meaning after writing the code.

Give every state a way out

Builders naturally plan forward. Users move forward, backward, sideways, and sometimes leave.

For each state, name one safe exit:

- edit the current input;
- cancel before the action;
- return to the prior step;
- reset after the result;
- retry after failure; or
- leave with an honest warning about what will be lost.

You do not need a complex navigation system. You need to avoid trapping the person inside a state they did not intend.

A safe exit also protects testing. If every test requires deleting the project or refreshing hidden state, the path is difficult to prove. A visible reset gives the tester a known start and makes repeated checks comparable.

Walk the exit from every important state before calling the path complete.

Preserve path evidence

Save more than a screenshot of the final state.

A useful path record contains:

- the starting state;
- the exact task;
- the inputs used;
- the states observed in order;
- the final result;
- any intervention or hidden setup;
- the build version or checkpoint; and
- failed or unproved boundaries.

The record makes later comparison possible. When Chapter 12 changes one behavior, you can rerun the same path and see whether the result improved without losing what already worked.

A screen can look identical while storage, access, or network behavior changes beneath it. Keep the behavior record and changed-file report together.

Practice Loop

The constructed Practice Loop case begins as a new local browser project.

The constructed path is:

1. The user enters a practice focus.
2. The user states what will count as finished.
3. The product creates one small plan.
4. The user leaves to practice.
5. The user returns and chooses `Completed`, `Partly completed`, or `Did not happen`.
6. The product shows the original intention and recorded outcome together.

The named states are:

- `Start`
- `Plan ready`
- `Outcome choices`
- `Result recorded`
- `Invalid input`
- `Reset`

The prototype handles one plan at a time. It does not save after refresh. A visible note states that closing or refreshing resets the current version.

The agent implements the path in small cycles. After each cycle, it runs the mapped checks and reports the changed files.

The builder runs the path in a browser before keeping the result.

Blank and whitespace-only input are blocked, and the user deliberately opens the outcome choices after creating a plan. Those checks pass. They do not show whether a new user understands when to record an outcome. Chapter 11 tests that separate question.

This is a constructed case. No account, public host, or real user information enters the first build.

Do It for Your App

Write the path before asking the agent to implement it.

```
PATH NAME

ENTRY
What tells the First User where to begin?

INPUT
What minimum information is required?

ACTION
What does the user do?

RESULT
What visible state proves the useful result exists?

RETURN
What can the user do next?

EXIT
How can the user cancel, reset, or leave safely?

REPEAT FOR EACH IMPORTANT STATE
State:
What the user sees:
Allowed action:
Next state:
Failure or limit:
```

Do not let the agent invent state names that make unsupported claims. `Payment confirmed` must mean the official payment system confirmed it. `Request sent` must mean the request actually left the product. `Saved` must mean the information can be found after the behavior you disclosed.

Next, break the implementation into vertical cycles.

Example:

1. Entry, approved input, and first visible state.
2. Main action and useful result.
3. Blank, repeat, cancel, and reset behavior.
4. Clarity, accessibility basics, checks, and final report.

Ask the agent to implement one cycle at a time.

```
Implement Cycle 1 only from the approved path and Build Brief.
Run the mapped checks. Report the behavior, changed files, results,
assumptions, and remaining cycles. Stop before Cycle 2.
```

At every stop, run the behavior yourself.

Ask the agent to name the file or local preview address to open and explain how to reopen it after the session ends. A local preview runs on your computer; it is not a public deployment. If a small local server is needed, have the agent explain and start the approved setup, then open the exact address it reports.

Do not accept a screenshot from the agent as your run. Open the app in your own browser. If it does not open, give the agent the exact error and keep the cycle unfinished. Record the working opening instructions in `BUILD-LOG.md` so the next session can start from the same place.

Do not test only the route you expect. Try to misunderstand the first instruction. Enter nothing. Repeat the main action. Use back. Reset from the middle. Resize the window. Use only the keyboard for the main path.

Record the result as pass, fail, or unproved.

```
Check:
Expected behavior:
Observed behavior:
Result: Pass | Fail | Unproved
Evidence:
```

An unproved check means the evidence does not exist yet. A required check must pass before you accept the cycle; unproved is not a substitute for pass.

Keep the build only when the approved cycle passes. If a change crosses the Scope Box, revert or revise before continuing.

When all cycles pass, perform one clean run from the starting state without using developer knowledge or hidden steps.

The Working Path is complete when the First User can create the promised result and every visible limit is true.

Prove It

Your Working Path passes this chapter when:

- one path connects entry, action, result, return, and exit;
- every important state is named;
- the result shows what happened, not a generic success message;
- likely failures and reset behavior have been run; and
- the path stays inside the approved Scope Box.

Your Result

Save the **Working Path** and its state list.

In Chapter 10, you will decide what information the app should forget, keep on one device, or place behind an account.

Chapter 10: Decide What the App Remembers

The Move

Remember only what the promise requires.

With unQbd, I use accounts, libraries, access, and reading progress because the product must recognize people and continue experiences over time.

Each remembered state creates responsibility.

I still have to decide what each state means, where it belongs, who can see it, how it changes, what happens when access fails, and how a person can remove information.

Your first app may not need that system.

Do not add storage or an account because products usually have them. Decide what the First User must find later for the Outcome Promise to remain true.

Your result is one **Data Decision**.

Why It Matters

Data changes the product even when the screen looks the same.

A plan that disappears after refresh is temporary. A plan that returns may be stored in the browser or fetched from a service. A plan available on another device needs a way to move or share the data. The screen alone cannot tell you which system exists.

Remember only what the promise requires.

Those are different promises.

Use three memory levels.

Temporary

Information exists only during the current session or current page state.

This is the simplest level. It can support a quick local test. The product must say that refresh, close, or restart clears the information when that is true.

Temporary does not mean unimportant. It means the product promises no return.

This device

Information stays in the browser or device.

This can support a small personal tool without an account. It also creates questions:

- Which browser and device contain the information?
- What happens in private browsing?
- Can another person using the device see it?

- How does the user delete it?
- What happens when browser data is cleared?
- Does the product still work offline?

Local browser storage is convenient. It is not a secure vault for secrets or sensitive records.

Account

Information is associated with an identity and can follow the user.

An account does not add synchronization by itself. Shared storage, access rules, and recovery must be built and checked too.

An account introduces sign-up, sign-in, sign-out, authorization, recovery, deletion, security, support, and often email or another identity provider.

It can also introduce a server, database, network dependency, privacy policy, and operating cost.

An account may become the right choice. It is not the default reward for finishing a local prototype.

Start with the minimum record

List every piece of information the app wants to remember.

For each item, ask:

1. Does the promise require it later?
2. What is the smallest useful form?
3. How long must it remain?
4. Who can see or change it?
5. How can the user remove it?
6. What happens if it is missing, stale, or wrong?

If the promise does not require the item, do not collect it.

Data minimization is not only a privacy idea. It reduces fields, states, bugs, support, and explanation.

Name the source of truth

A visible screen may show a copy of information stored elsewhere.

If the screen and stored record disagree, which one wins?

For a one-device app, the browser record may be the source of truth. For payment, the hosted payment provider is the source of truth, not your success screen. For account access, the maintained identity and entitlement system is the source of truth.

Write the answer. Do not let the interface become truth by appearance.

Remembering includes deletion

If the product can save information, the product needs a way to explain and remove it.

Deletion should be visible, intentional, and testable. The user should know what will be removed and whether the action affects one item, all local information, or an account.

After deletion, refresh and restart. Confirm the information does not return.

A fake delete button is worse than no save feature because it creates a false promise.

Do not store secrets in the product

Passwords, private keys, payment credentials, service tokens, and administrative credentials do not belong in browser code, public project files, screenshots, prompts, or ordinary data records.

Use approved maintained services for sensitive functions. Give the agent public identifiers or safe placeholders only when required.

If the product cannot protect the information, change the path so it does not collect the information.

Do not confuse a record with a history

Saving the current result is not the same as building a history.

A current record answers, "What is true now?" A history answers, "What happened across several points in time?"

History creates more decisions:

- which events are kept;
- whether an old value can be edited;
- which time and time zone apply;
- how duplicates are handled;
- how long records remain;
- whether deletion removes one item or all items; and
- what the product is allowed to infer from the pattern.

If the Outcome Promise needs only the current plan and most recent result, do not add charts, streaks, or a permanent log. Those features can change the product from a simple planning tool into a behavior-tracking system.

Make history earn its responsibility.

Test the memory from the user's position

The builder knows where data lives. The user sees only what returns.

Run memory tests through the same actions the user can take:

1. create the record;
2. leave the current state;
3. return in the way the disclosure describes;
4. change the record;
5. remove it;
6. repeat the return; and
7. confirm the old value does not reappear.

If the product is used on a shared device, ask what the next person in the same browser profile will see. If the answer is the prior user's data, the interface and offer must not imply personal privacy.

If the product uses an account, test signed out, wrong account, expired access, recovery, and deletion. Those are not minor additions. They are why an account belongs behind a separate architecture and trust decision.

The memory level should make the product easier to rely on, not merely harder to lose.

Let the Data Decision shape the offer

Data behavior becomes part of what a buyer receives.

A one-device product can be useful, but the offer should not imply that work follows the buyer everywhere. A temporary product can support a guided demonstration, but it should not be sold as a long-term record. An account product can support shared access, but only when authorization and recovery match the claim.

Write one buyer-facing limit beside the technical decision:

> *Because this version uses ____________ memory, the buyer should expect ____________ and should not expect ____________.*

This sentence will reappear in the Trust Map, Offer One-Pager, and Buyer Path. Keeping it now prevents the sales language from promising a larger data system than the product built.

Practice Loop

The constructed Practice Loop case reaches Chapter 10 with a complete local path and no persistence.

The first test needs to observe whether the path makes sense. It does not yet need a long-term record or several devices.

The Data Decision is:

Information	Memory level now	Reason
Practice focus	Temporary	Needed only for the current local path.
Completion definition	Temporary	Needed to judge the current result.
Outcome choice	Temporary	Shown beside the current intention.
Name, email, or identity	Not collected	Not required by the promise.
History	Not collected	Not required by the first test.

The product says:

> *This local prototype does not save your plan. Refreshing or closing the page resets it.*

That limit may frustrate a tester. The frustration becomes evidence. It does not justify storage before the test happens.

The case defers local persistence until the trust work can include disclosure, deletion, and recovery checks.

This is a constructed teaching decision.

Do It for Your App

Create a data inventory for the Working Path.

```
Information item:
Why the promise requires it:
Minimum useful form:
Memory level: Temporary | This device | Account | Do not collect
Source of truth:
Who can see it:
Who can change it:
Retention or reset rule:
Deletion method:
Missing, stale, or wrong behavior:
```

Do not group unrelated information under `user data`. A name, payment status, saved plan, access role, and support message have different jobs and risks.

Now choose the lowest memory level that keeps the promise true.

If temporary works, use temporary for the first test.

If the result must survive refresh on the same device, consider device-only storage with clear limits and deletion.

If the result must follow an identity, be shared, or control paid access, an account may be required. Treat that as a larger product decision and a deeper review boundary.

Write the user disclosure in ordinary language:

```
This product stores __________ in __________.
It does not __________.
You can remove it by __________.
If you refresh, close, switch device, or lose access, __________
happens.
```

Avoid broad claims such as `secure` or `private` without a precise meaning and proof.

Then update the Build Brief.

For temporary data:

```
CHOOSE THE APPROVED MEMORY LEVEL ONLY

TEMPORARY
Keep data only in the current page state, with no saved copy.
Show the reset behavior before the user depends on it.

THIS DEVICE
Store only the approved fields in this browser on this device.
Add a clear action to delete this app's local data. Prove deletion
across refresh.
Do not add an account, external network request, or sync.
```

For account data, stop the simple build and write a separate trust and architecture decision before implementation. Do not let the agent create an identity system as a side effect of another task.

Map the checks:

- create the approved record;
- refresh or restart as disclosed;
- change the record;
- enter blank and long values;
- use a shared or private-browsing scenario when relevant;
- delete the record;
- refresh again; and
- confirm removed information does not return.

Check the network if the promise says information stays local.

Finally, read the data decision as the user. The person should know what is remembered before relying on it.

Prove It

Your Data Decision passes this chapter when:

- every collected item supports the Outcome Promise;
- the lowest responsible memory level is chosen;
- the source of truth and deletion path are named;
- the user-facing disclosure matches actual behavior; and
- secrets and unnecessary personal information remain outside the product and prompts.

Your Result

Save the **Data Decision** and update the Build Brief.

In Chapter 11, you will watch a real person use the Working Path and record behavior before explaining it.

Chapter 11: Watch Someone Use It

The Move

Watch behavior without teaching the product.

When I look at an unQbd screen, I carry the company in my head. I know what the words mean, where the next path leads, and what I intended each control to do.

A new reader has none of that context.

The person sees only the current screen.

If I explain the path while the person uses it, I am testing my explanation. I am not testing the product.

Your move is to give one real task, remain quiet, and record what the person does before you decide why it happened.

Your result is one **Observation Note**.

Why It Matters

User testing is not a vote on whether the app looks good.

It is a way to compare your intended path with another person's real behavior.

Keep three evidence types separate:

- **Did:** an observable action.
- **Said:** the person's actual words.
- **Builder inference:** your explanation of the action or comment.

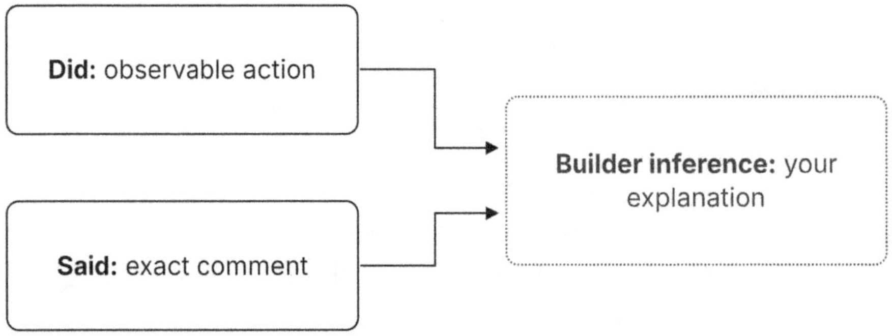

Observation and interpretation are not the same thing.

Only the first two come directly from the session.

Example:

> ***Did:*** *The person selected the result before leaving to practice.* ***Said:*** *"Am I supposed to choose this now?"* ***Inference:*** *The product makes future and completed states look available together.*

The inference may be correct. Keeping it separate makes the next change easier to challenge.

Give a task, not instructions

Weak task:

> *Enter a focus in the top box, click Create Plan, read the note, then click the return button.*

That is a guided demonstration.

Stronger task:

> *Use this product to plan one short practice session and later record what happened.*

The second task describes the intended outcome. The product must communicate the path.

Use a clean starting state

Start with the same state a real first user would see.

Remove old sample data unless the public product will include it. Do not leave the app in a convenient internal state. Use the same device size, browser, access, and disclosure the user will receive.

If the test depends on a hidden setup step, the path is not ready.

Remain quiet

Silence feels uncomfortable when someone hesitates.

Do not point, finish the person's sentence, rename the control, or say what you expected. If the person asks a question, respond with:

> *What would you do if I were not here?*

Intervene for safety, privacy, an irreversible action, or a clear test boundary. End the task if the person wants to stop. You are observing the product, not testing the person's patience.

Record the intervention because it changed the session.

Comments and behavior can disagree

A person can say the product is easy after getting lost. Another person can complete the path and say the design feels plain.

Both comments matter. They answer different questions.

Use behavior to judge whether the path worked. Use comments to find expectations, language, trust concerns, and value questions.

Do not replace observed completion with politeness.

Test the right person

The tester should fit the First User description closely enough that the task is real.

A supportive friend outside the problem can find interface confusion. That person cannot validate the product need.

Record the fit:

- why this person fits the First User;
- the relevant current method; and
- what is different from the intended user.

Protect the person

Use safe sample information. Do not ask a tester to expose private messages, credentials, payment details, health information, or another person's data.

For a local prototype, use a known person and a device you can reset. If you are under 18, use the approved adult and cohort process.

Observation does not require surveillance. You need the path, actions, comments, and result.

Before starting, explain what you will observe and what notes you will keep. Ask the person to agree. Ask separately before recording audio, video, or the screen, and use notes alone when recording is unnecessary. The person can stop at any time.

Do not turn the session into feature voting

At the end of a test, people often suggest what to add.

Write the request down. Then return to the behavior behind it.

A request for reminders may mean the person forgot to return. It may mean the result is not important enough to remember. It may mean the product promises a habit system even though you intended a one-session planner.

A request for a dashboard may mean the current result is hard to find. It may also mean the participant imagines a different user, such as an instructor.

Ask:

- What happened that made you want that feature?
- What would you do if the feature did not exist?
- Which result would the feature help you create?

The answers belong in the Observation Note. The requested mechanism stays separate.

Record successful behavior too

Testing can become a search for problems. That creates another risk: the next change breaks what already worked.

Record positive behavior with the same precision:

- the participant found the starting point without help;
- the label produced the expected action;
- the person understood the result state;
- reset returned to a known beginning; or
- the disclosure changed the person's expectation.

These are not compliments. They are behaviors the next change should preserve.

Add one line to every Observation Note: **Behavior that worked and must not regress:**

Use a second observer carefully

A second observer can catch behavior you miss. The observers should still produce one clean record.

Before the session, assign jobs. One person can watch the path and timing. The other can capture short statements and interventions. Neither should coach.

After the session, compare notes before discussing causes. If one observer wrote, "The participant was confused," ask what visible action supports it. Replace the label with the action.

Disagreement can remain. Record Observer A's inference, Observer B's inference, the shared observed behavior, and the next evidence that could distinguish them.

The shared behavior is stronger than either story.

Know when one session is enough to stop

Repeated behavior gives ordinary usability findings more weight. Some failures do not need repetition before action.

Stop the session when the product exposes private information, performs an irreversible action without approval, creates a charge, publishes unexpectedly, traps the user, or makes a harmful claim.

One serious event can block release. Record the exact state and preserve evidence safely. Do not ask another person to repeat a dangerous action merely to increase the count.

Choose the number of sessions for the decision

There is no magic number that proves an interface works for everyone.

Use enough sessions to support the next bounded decision.

One session can expose a serious trust blocker. Several relevant sessions can show whether an ordinary path barrier repeats. A new audience, device, language, or access need may require another group because the prior sessions did not cover it.

Stop adding sessions when the current evidence already points to one clear bounded change. More observation does not help if the builder refuses to act on the repeated barrier.

Continue observing when the notes conflict, the tester did not fit the First User, coaching changed the result, or the product state was not consistent.

Record why the current set is enough for the next move and what it cannot represent.

Practice Loop

Practice Loop uses three constructed usability sessions.

Each participant is an adult hobby learner. Each receives the task:

> *Use this local product to plan one short practice session and record what happened.*

The observations are:

Session	Did	Said	Evidence weight
1	Created a plan, then immediately opened the result controls.	"Am I supposed to choose this now?"	High. Premature reporting is easy.
2	Created a plan, paused, then asked whether the plan was already recorded as done.	"Did that finish it?"	High. Plan and result states are unclear.
3	Followed the intended sequence, refreshed, and lost the plan.	"I thought it would still be here."	Serious known limit. The visible disclosure did not prevent the expectation.

The builder records two different problems.

The first two sessions show a state-clarity barrier in the main path. The third shows that temporary data may not fit expectations.

The builder does not fix both in one change.

State clarity affects the promised sequence and appears twice. Refresh behavior becomes an input to the trust and recovery work.

These sessions are constructed teaching evidence. They are not real unQbd research.

Do It for Your App

Prepare one observation session.

```
FIRST USER FIT
Why this person fits:

STARTING STATE
What the person will see first:

TASK
One outcome statement, with no click instructions:

SAFETY BOUNDARY
What data, account, payment, public action, or irreversible action
is excluded:

STOP CONDITION
When I will intervene:

SUCCESS BEHAVIOR
What completion looks like:
```

Create an observation sheet:

```
Time or step:
Did:
Said:
Intervention:
Result:
Builder inference after the session:
```

Run the session without coaching.

Watch for:

- the first place the person looks;
- the first action;
- hesitation;
- backtracking;
- repeated actions;
- misunderstood state;
- information the person expects;
- attempts to leave, cancel, or reset;
- the point where the useful result becomes clear; and
- the point where the person believes the task is complete.

After the task, ask a few short questions:

- What did you think would happen before you started?
- What did you think happened at the end?
- Which moment felt unclear?
- What would you do next if I were not here?
- What did you expect the product to remember?

Do not add "Would you pay?" to a usability session and treat the answer as a buyer decision. Offer evidence comes later through a real choice.

Repeat with at least two more relevant people when safe and reachable. A repeated barrier deserves more weight than one preference. A single serious trust or safety failure can still block release.

Now group the notes without erasing differences.

```
Repeated main-path barrier:
Single serious barrier:
Expectation mismatch:
Preference only:
Positive behavior that should not be broken:
Unknown requiring another test:
```

Choose one barrier for Chapter 12. Do not choose the easiest cosmetic comment if a repeated main-path barrier exists.

Prove It

Your Observation Note passes this chapter when:

- the tester fits the First User or the mismatch is disclosed;
- the task describes an outcome rather than clicks;
- Did, Said, and inference remain separate;
- interventions are recorded; and
- one barrier is chosen from behavior, not founder preference.

Your Result

Save the **Observation Note** and the selected barrier.

In Chapter 12, you will make one bounded change, retest it, and leave unrelated feedback outside the cycle.

Chapter 12: Fix the Smallest Real Barrier

The Move

Fix the barrier blocking the promised path.

During the unQbd iOS release process, a reviewer hit a login loop. Trying to reach full content sent the reviewer back to login.

The product had many other things I could improve. None mattered while access returned the user to the same blocked state.

The right next move was not a broader redesign. It was to remove the real barrier, verify the access path, and resubmit the corrected build.

Your Observation Note gives you the same kind of choice.

Select one barrier, make one bounded change, and retest the same path.

Your result is one **Change Decision**.

Why It Matters

Feedback creates a pile.

One tester wants a new feature. Another dislikes a label. A third expects saved data. You notice a spacing issue. The agent suggests cleanup. The product suddenly has a backlog instead of a decision.

Rank findings by their effect on the Outcome Promise.

Use this order:

1. **Trust or safety blocker:** the product can harm, expose, mislead, charge, publish, or act without the required control.
2. **Main-path blocker:** the First User cannot create the promised result.
3. **Repeated state or language barrier:** several relevant users misunderstand the same important step.

4. **Serious expectation mismatch:** the product technically works but creates a false belief about data, access, payment, or result.
5. **Preference or polish:** the path works and the feedback concerns taste or convenience.

One serious trust blocker can outrank repeated minor confusion.

Fix the behavior, not the comment

A tester may say, "Add a progress bar."

The observed problem may be that the user cannot tell whether the task started, is waiting, or finished.

The progress bar is one suggested mechanism. The behavior to fix is state clarity.

Write the barrier without the requested feature:

> *When the user ____________, the product ____________, so the user cannot ____________.*

This keeps the agent from implementing the first suggestion without understanding the problem.

Change one variable

If you change the label, sequence, storage, layout, and navigation together, a successful retest will not tell you which change mattered.

Choose the smallest change likely to remove the barrier. Preserve everything that already worked.

The change can still involve several files. One variable means one product hypothesis, not one line of code.

Define the retest before the edit

Write the expected behavior and failure condition before the agent changes the product.

Name the current observed barrier, one change hypothesis, the behavior expected after the change, the behavior that would show failure, and the existing behavior that must not regress.

The retest should use the same starting state and task when possible. A different task produces different evidence.

Keep deferred findings visible

Not fixing a finding does not require forgetting it.

Use four buckets:

- fix now;
- test again before deciding;
- defer until the next product boundary; and
- reject because it conflicts with the promise or evidence.

Every finding gets a reason. The list does not control the product. The current constraint does.

Recheck the whole path

A small change can create a regression.

After the focused retest passes, rerun the full Working Path. Test the boundary states affected by the change. Review the changed files and the agent's assumptions.

Do not keep a local fix that breaks reset, data behavior, keyboard use, or another required state.

A barrier can reveal a wrong product decision

Not every barrier belongs in the interface.

Suppose the tester cannot complete the path because the product requires information they do not have. A clearer label will not fix a wrong input requirement.

Suppose the buyer expects another person to approve the action. Faster navigation will not fix the Buyer Map.

Suppose the person refuses because the product saves information they do not want stored. The issue may belong in the Data Decision and Trust Map.

Before editing, ask which earlier decision owns the barrier:

- **Problem:** Is this the real broken moment?
- **User or buyer:** Is the test person able to use and approve the path?
- **Promise:** Is the result narrow and controllable?
- **Scope:** Did another product enter?
- **Data:** Does memory match the expectation?
- **Interface:** Is the intended behavior merely unclear?

Return to the earlier chapter when the barrier points there. Do not use interface polish to protect a wrong assumption.

Set a change budget

One hypothesis can still invite a large implementation.

Before approving the plan, set a budget in the units that matter:

- one product behavior;
- named files or components;
- no new dependency or service;
- one focused test and one full-path regression; and
- one retest before another change.

The budget is not a line-count target. A small behavior can require several correct file changes. The point is to keep the experiment readable.

If the agent discovers that the fix requires a new data system, account, provider, or product role, stop the work order. That discovery is evidence that the hypothesis crossed a boundary.

Write the discovery into the Change Decision. You may revise the brief, choose a simpler fix, return to an earlier decision, or stop.

Preserve the rejected idea

A rejected feature can return later as if no decision was made.

Record the requested idea, observed behavior behind it, decision to defer, reject, or test later, reason, and evidence that would reopen it.

This keeps the backlog from becoming a waiting room where every idea eventually enters the product.

Keep the retest comparable

A retest should change the product behavior, not the surrounding conditions.

Keep these items as stable as practical:

- First User fit;
- starting state;
- task wording;
- device and screen size;
- data and account state;
- amount of observer help; and
- success behavior.

If a condition must change, record it. A better result on a larger screen with the founder explaining the new label does not prove the change works independently.

Use a new relevant participant when you want to test whether the revised interface communicates without prior coaching. Use the original participant when the decision is specifically whether that person's barrier was removed. The two tests answer different questions.

After the retest, compare the prior and revised behavior. Name the product change, any change in test conditions, any regression, and the final decision and limit.

Keep a change only when the evidence supports the hypothesis at the size you claimed. One clean retest can earn the next trust cycle. It cannot prove the product is easy for everyone.

Record who accepted the decision and when. The agent can maintain the file, but it should not silently mark its own work accepted. A short line such as `Kept after human retest on [date]` prevents a future session from treating an implemented experiment as an approved product decision. If the result remains disputed, write that too and keep the checkpoint.

Practice Loop

The constructed Practice Loop case has two repeated observations:

- one participant opened result controls immediately after creating the plan; and
- one participant could not tell whether creating the plan meant practice was finished.

The selected barrier is:

> *After a plan is created, the product does not clearly distinguish leaving to practice from opening the outcome choices, so the user may report too early.*

The one change hypothesis is:

- show `Practice first. Return when you are ready to record what happened.` after plan creation;
- keep result choices hidden;
- reveal them only after the user chooses `I am back from practice`.

The change does not add storage. The lost-on-refresh observation remains deferred to the trust work.

The earlier control already hid the choices until the user opened them. The revised message and return label explain when to take that action. They do not detect practice or prevent someone from reporting early. Practice Loop records a self-report, not verified activity.

In a constructed retest, a fourth adult hobby learner creates the plan, reads the new instruction, leaves the result choices closed, chooses `I am back from practice`, and records an outcome.

That retest supports the revised state sequence for one participant. It does not prove universal ease, long-term value, or willingness to pay.

The case records the result as keep for the next trust cycle.

Do It for Your App

Choose the highest-ranked barrier from Chapter 11.

Complete the Change Card:

```
OBSERVED BARRIER
What did the person do?
What did the person say?

EVIDENCE WEIGHT
Trust blocker | Main-path blocker | Repeated barrier |
Expectation mismatch | Preference

ONE CHANGE HYPOTHESIS
What single product behavior should change?

RETEST
Starting state:
Task:
Expected behavior:
Failure behavior:

REGRESSION CHECK
What already works and must remain true?

DEFERRED FINDINGS
What stays outside this cycle, and why?

AFTER RETEST
Prior behavior:
Revised behavior:
Product change:
Test-condition change:
Regression found:
Decision and evidence limit:
```

Update the Build Brief and Agent Work Order with the Change Card.

Ask the agent to inspect before editing:

```
Review the Observation Note, Change Card, current source, and
tests.
Explain the smallest change that tests the hypothesis.
List expected files, focused checks, regression checks, and
assumptions.
Do not edit yet. Do not include deferred findings.
```

Reject a plan that bundles cleanup, new features, data changes, or style work unrelated to the barrier.

After plan approval, create a checkpoint and implement the change.

Run the focused checks first. If they fail, inspect the result before adding another change. Do not stack guesses.

Then run the full path and important boundaries.

Conduct the retest with a relevant person who has not been coached on the new behavior. Use the same task. Record Did, Said, and inference separately.

Choose one decision:

Keep

The barrier is removed, the main path passes, and no important regression appears.

Revise

The hypothesis remains plausible, but the behavior is still unclear. Write one new bounded hypothesis.

Revert

The change does not remove the barrier or creates a more serious problem.

Stop

The barrier reveals that the promise, user, data decision, or responsibility is wrong for the project.

Record what the retest proves and what it does not prove.

Prove It

Your Change Decision passes this chapter when:

- the selected barrier comes from observed behavior;
- one product hypothesis controls the change;
- the retest was defined before implementation;
- the focused and full-path checks were run; and
- keep, revise, revert, or stop is supported by the retest.

Your Result

Save the **Change Decision** and the updated Working Path.

In Chapter 13, you will draw the product's trust boundary and decide what must be fixed before another person can rely on it.

Part IV: Make It Safe and Sellable

Chapter 13: Draw the Trust Boundary

The Move

Decide what your product is allowed to know and do.

An app may look small while carrying a large responsibility. A form can collect private information. A button can charge money. A saved record can appear to belong to one person while anyone using the device can see it.

The AI agent can build each of those behaviors quickly. That does not mean you should approve them.

With unQbd, I cannot use one trust rule for every part of the product. Public book information is different from a member's account. Reading progress is different from a payment. Content for a child deserves a different level of care from a public marketing page.

Before another person relies on your app, draw the line around its responsibility.

Your result is one **Trust Map**.

Why It Matters

The trust boundary is the edge of the promise you are prepared to protect.

Inside that boundary are the information, actions, people, and claims your product accepts responsibility for. Outside it are the things your current version does not collect, perform, or promise.

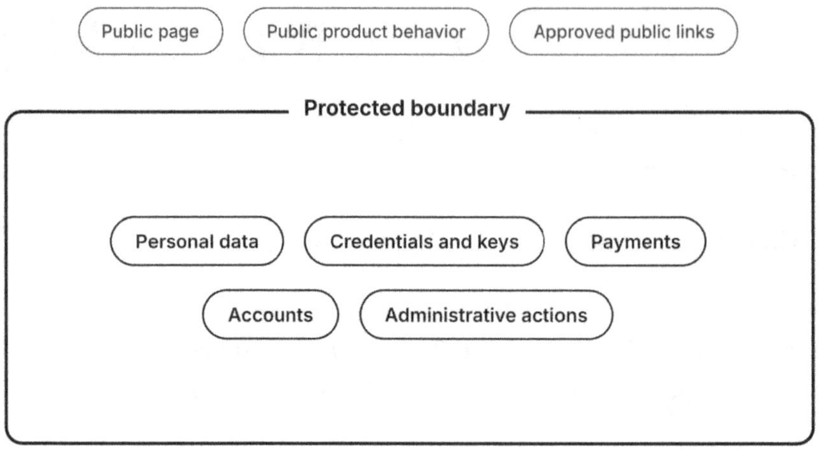

If the product cannot protect it, do not collect it.

This is not a legal document or a security audit. It is a founder's first control over a product that AI can expand faster than the founder can understand it.

Map five things

You can draw a useful Trust Map with five questions.

1. **What enters?** List information a person types, selects, uploads, or connects.
2. **What stays?** List what the app saves, where it stays, and how long it remains.
3. **What leaves?** List information sent across a network, shared with a service, emailed, published, or exported.
4. **Who can act?** List who can view, change, delete, approve, charge, publish, or administer something.
5. **What does the product claim?** List what the person may believe about privacy, accuracy, access, safety, or results.

If you cannot answer one of these questions, mark it unknown. Do not let the agent fill the gap with a convenient default.

Collect less

The safest information is often the information you never collect.

Return to the Outcome Promise. Ask what the product truly needs for that one result.

A practice-planning app may need the activity and a description of what counts as finished. It probably does not need a legal name, birth date, precise location, contact list, or microphone access.

An AI agent may suggest accounts because accounts are common. That does not make an account necessary. An account adds identity, passwords or sign-in providers, recovery, deletion, access control, and support. One familiar feature can quietly create six new responsibilities.

Delete fields that do not earn their risk.

Know where saved data lives

"Saved" is not a complete answer.

Data can live only in the current page, in the browser on one device, in a file, or in an online account. Each choice creates a different expectation.

Local browser storage can be appropriate for a narrow first version. It can also be misunderstood. Local does not mean secret. Another person using the same browser profile may be able to see the information. Clearing browser data may remove it. It does not sync to another device unless you build that behavior.

Tell the user what the product actually does in plain language.

For example:

> *This version stores your current plan and recent result in this browser on this device. It does not create an account or sync across devices. You can delete the local data inside the app.*

That statement is a product requirement. The build, test, and interface must all agree with it.

When adding persistence, use a consistent local preview address. Do not rely on storage tests made by double-clicking a file; browser behavior for `file:` addresses is not guaranteed.

Browser storage belongs to an **origin**, the address's protocol, host, and port. Changing any of those can give the app a different storage area, even in the same browser. Ask the agent to record the tested address and reopening steps. A public address will have its own data; it will not inherit the local prototype's plan.

The browser can also refuse to save data. Test that case and show an honest message instead of `Saved`. Chapter 14 adds the recovery behavior.

Separate public, personal, and controlled actions

Not every screen needs the same control.

A public description can be visible to anyone. A person's saved entry should not automatically be public. An administrative action should not be available merely because someone knows a hidden web address.

Use three simple labels:

- **Public:** safe and intended for anyone to see.
- **Personal:** belongs to the user or device and needs clear access and deletion behavior.
- **Controlled:** changes another person's access, money, data, publication, or account and needs stronger authorization and review.

If your first version does not need a controlled action, remove it. Do not hide it and call that security.

Treat output as input too

Your app may display text a user entered or content an AI generated. That output can still create problems.

Text that looks like code should normally appear as text unless the product explicitly needs to run it. A blank entry should not create a broken record. An extremely long entry should not destroy the layout. Generated advice should not be presented as a guaranteed fact merely because it sounds confident.

The product should also work for people who use a keyboard, need visible focus, enlarge text, or use a phone-sized screen. Accessibility is part of whether a person can trust the promised path.

Make deletion real

If you save personal information, give the user an understandable way to remove it when the product can support that honestly.

Do not add a button labeled Delete and assume the job is finished. Test that the data disappears, stays gone after refresh, and does not silently return from another source.

If complete deletion requires an account request or support action, say so. The label should match the behavior.

Stop at the boundary

Some products carry more responsibility than a beginner project should accept.

Pause before collecting sensitive health, financial, educational, employment, precise location, identity, or private information. Pause before handling money directly, making decisions about another person, or giving advice that could cause serious harm.

You may be able to reduce the responsibility. Use a hosted payment page instead of handling card details. Use a public information source instead of storing a copy. Let an adult own the account for a youth-facing offer. Remove the sensitive feature from the first version.

The smallest responsible product is better than the largest product you cannot protect.

Make every unknown visible

A Trust Map does not need to make every uncertainty disappear. It needs to stop uncertainty from becoming an invisible promise.

Use three labels:

- **Known:** you inspected and tested the actual behavior.
- **Assumed:** the product or agent appears to behave this way, but the proof is incomplete.
- **Outside:** this version refuses the responsibility.

An assumed item cannot support a strong public claim. If you have not verified whether data leaves the device, do not say it never leaves. If deletion has not been tested after refresh, do not say the information is gone.

Move the item to known through evidence, move it outside by removing the behavior, or stop before another person relies on it.

Honest uncertainty is a product control.

Practice Loop

In the constructed Practice Loop case, this chapter begins with a working local path and one deferred problem: refresh destroys the current plan.

The proposed Trust Map for the persistence change says:

Question	Bounded answer
What enters?	Practice focus, completion description, and one outcome choice
What stays?	Current plan and most recent result in this browser on this device
What leaves?	Nothing in this version
Who can act?	The person using this browser profile
What is claimed?	Plan one practice session and record what happened

The review repeats the blank and whitespace checks from Chapter 9. Required-input validation already passes and must remain intact.

Two related requirements now block offering a saved-plan product:

1. the current plan and result must survive refresh in the supported browser; and
2. the user must be able to delete that saved local data.

The bounded trust change adds local browser persistence, the plain-language local-data statement, and `Delete local data`. It preserves the validated inputs and revised outcome sequence.

The saved outcome remains attached to the plan it describes. Starting another plan must not carry forward the previous plan's completion status.

The test confirms that deleted data does not return after refresh. The delete action removes only this app's stored items. HTML-like input displays as text both when entered and when restored. The app still makes no external network request and adds no account, tracking, notification, cloud database, or cross-device sync.

Local persistence solves one expectation. It does not make the data private from other people using the same browser profile. These findings and fixes are teaching inputs, not results from a released product.

Do It for Your App

Start with the exact Working Path you kept in Chapter 12.

Complete this Trust Map:

```
PROMISE
What exact result does the product claim to create?

WHAT ENTERS
What can a person type, choose, upload, or connect?

WHAT STAYS
What is saved? Where? For how long?

WHAT LEAVES
What is transmitted, shared, emailed, published, or exported?

WHO CAN ACT
Who can view, change, delete, approve, charge, publish, or
administer?

PLAIN-LANGUAGE DISCLOSURE
What must the user understand before relying on the product?

OUTSIDE THIS VERSION
What data, action, or claim will the product refuse?
```

Mark each item public, personal, or controlled. Circle every unknown.

Now compare the map with the current product. Look for disagreements:

- the interface collects more than the promise needs;
- the product saves data without saying where;
- the disclosure says local but the product sends a network request;

- the app says delete but the information returns;
- a user can reach an action they should not control; or
- the product implies a result the evidence cannot support.

Choose the smallest set of release blockers. A blocker is not every possible improvement. It is a mismatch that makes the promised path unsafe, inaccessible, misleading, or unreliable.

Give the AI agent a bounded trust review:

```
Inspect the Trust Map, Build Brief, current product, and tests.
Do not edit yet.
List every mismatch between the stated boundary and actual
behavior.
Separate release blockers from later improvements.
Propose the smallest fix set and the checks that would prove each
fix.
Do not add an account, service, dependency, network action, or new
feature.
```

Review the answer yourself. A security-sounding report is not proof. Ask the agent to show where data enters, stays, leaves, and returns. Run the important behaviors.

At minimum, test blank input, long input, text that resembles markup, refresh, deletion, phone-sized layout, keyboard use, and the network behavior named by your brief.

If the boundary includes authentication, payment, uploaded files, private records, administrative control, or a public AI action, seek deeper technical review before release. The Trust Map helps you ask for the right review. It does not replace one.

Prove It

Your Trust Map passes this chapter when:

- the product collects only what the Outcome Promise needs;
- saved and transmitted data are named separately;
- access, deletion, and disclosure match actual behavior;
- public, personal, and controlled actions are separated; and
- every release blocker is fixed with a passing check, or the affected use stops.

Your Result

Save the **Trust Map** with the Build Brief.

In Chapter 14, you will decide what happens when the trusted path fails and how the user gets back to safety.

Chapter 14: Plan Failure, Recovery, and Support

The Move

Give the user a safe way back.

A product is not ready because the happy path works once. It becomes dependable when failure is understandable, recoverable, and owned.

This matters to me because unQbd is not one screen. A reader may need to sign in, open content, return later, manage access, or ask for help. If one handoff fails, the whole experience can feel broken even when every other part works.

Your first app may be much smaller. It still needs an answer to one basic question:

> *When something goes wrong, what can the person do next?*

Your result is one **Recovery Plan**.

Why It Matters

Most builders describe the product in verbs such as create, save, buy, send, or publish.

Users meet a second set of verbs: retry, cancel, return, restore, delete, contact, and leave.

Those recovery verbs are part of the product.

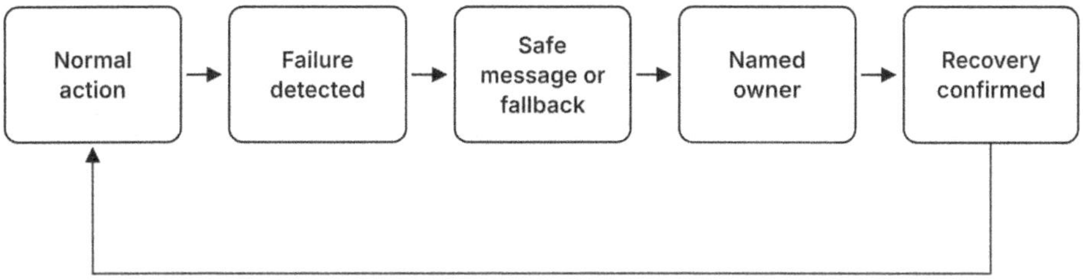

Recovery is part of the product.

Name the likely failures

Do not start with every failure in computing. Start with the promised path.

Walk through it one step at a time and ask:

- What if the input is missing or invalid?
- What if the action takes longer than expected?
- What if the device refreshes or closes?
- What if a service is unavailable?
- What if the user changes their mind?
- What if saved information is damaged or no longer understood?
- What if the product completes the action but the user cannot tell?

The answers create a short failure list tied to real behavior.

Use a recovery ladder

Choose the least expensive recovery that truly restores the person.

1. **Prevent:** block an invalid action before it creates damage.
2. **Explain:** state what happened in language the user understands.

3. **Retry:** let the person safely attempt the action again.
4. **Return:** preserve enough state to go back without starting over.
5. **Restore:** recover a known good state or copy of important data.
6. **Escalate:** provide a real support path when the product cannot recover itself.
7. **Stop safely:** end the action without charging, publishing, deleting, or corrupting something further.

Not every app needs all seven. Every important failure needs at least one honest next step.

Make error messages useful

"Something went wrong" describes the builder's uncertainty, not the user's next move.

A useful message answers three questions:

1. What did not happen?
2. What can the person do now?
3. Is their prior work safe?

For example:

> *Your plan was not saved. Your entries are still on this screen. Try again, or copy them before closing the page.*

Do not blame the user. Do not expose internal system details. Do not promise that data is safe unless you verified it.

Design actions that can be repeated safely

A retry should not create two purchases, two records, two messages, or two public posts.

The deeper technical term for this is not important here. The product rule is simple: when a user repeats an uncertain action, the result should be predictable.

Payment, publication, deletion, and invitations deserve special care. A button should show when work is in progress. Repeated clicks should not silently repeat a controlled action. The final state should be visible.

If your first version cannot guarantee this, use a simpler method. A hosted payment page, manual approval, draft state, or confirmation step may carry less risk than a custom automated flow.

Preserve a known good version

Recovery is also for the builder.

Before a meaningful change, preserve a checkpoint you know worked. Record what passed, not merely the date.

A useful checkpoint records the known-good behavior, checks that passed, files or version preserved, how to return, and what new data would be lost by returning.

The last line matters. Returning the code to an older version does not automatically restore data created after that version.

Decide who owns support

Support is part of the offer whether you planned it or not.

If a buyer cannot sign in, find the promised result, understand a charge, or remove their data, someone owns the next action. In a tiny business, that person may be you.

Write the support boundary before launch:

- where a person asks for help;
- what hours or response window you actually offer;
- which problems you can solve;
- which information you need without requesting unnecessary private data;
- when you refund, replace, restore, or stop; and
- what happens after the support window closes.

Do not promise instant support if no one is assigned to provide it.

Separate recovery from feature requests

A person who loses work needs recovery. A person who wants automatic reminders has a feature request.

Both may be valuable. They do not have the same urgency.

Use this order:

1. prevent harm or irreversible action;
2. restore the promised result;
3. explain the limit honestly;
4. reduce repeated support work; and
5. consider convenience features later.

This prevents a polished roadmap from hiding a broken path.

Test the failure on purpose

Do not wait for a customer to discover whether recovery works.

Enter bad data. Refresh at the wrong moment. Disconnect the network if the product claims offline behavior. Repeat an action. Cancel. Delete. Close and reopen. Use a copy of the project, not irreplaceable live data.

The test passes only when the product and the recovery message agree.

Count recovery as part of delivery

Recovery consumes real time.

If one in every few buyers needs a password reset, manual correction, refund, data restore, or setup rescue, that work belongs in the offer and price. It does not disappear because the app usually works.

Create a simple support record:

Record the failure, time to understand, time to recover, outside provider or cost, result, and change that could prevent a repeat.

Record the recovery even when you solve it in minutes. Small interruptions become expensive when they repeat, and memory usually understates how often the founder stepped in.

A short accurate log helps you distinguish three situations.

Rare failure with cheap recovery: keep the recovery and monitor it.

Repeated failure with the same cause: improve the product or instructions.

Failure that requires founder judgment every time: narrow the offer, charge for the work, create an operating procedure, or stop offering that path.

Do not automate the first recovery merely to hide the labor. Perform it safely, understand it, and then decide whether automation reduces a demonstrated cost.

This business reading happens later, but the measurement begins now.

Practice Loop

In the constructed Practice Loop case, the app now stores the current plan and most recent result in the local browser. The Trust Map tells the user exactly that.

The Recovery Plan tests five likely failures.

Failure	Safe response
Blank practice focus or completion description	Prevent plan creation and point to the missing field
Refresh during an active plan	Restore the current plan from local data
Browser refuses to save	Keep entries visible, explain that they are not saved, and let the user copy them before leaving
Local data cannot be read	Explain that the saved plan could not be restored; confirm before discarding it and starting empty
User chooses Delete local data	Confirm the action, remove local data, return to the empty state, and verify it stays gone after refresh

The builder preserved a known-good checkpoint before the storage change and creates another before recovery work. The builder then disconnects from the internet and tests the loaded local app. Its planning, recording, and local-data controls still work. Offline behavior is checked, not inferred from the absence of an online account.

The case does not add an online backup. It does not promise recovery after browser data is cleared. The disclosure states that limit.

If a user reports a problem during the small offer test, the founder owns the support reply. The first response asks what action the person took and what they saw. It does not ask for unrelated personal information. This Recovery Plan is a worked scenario, not support history from a live product.

Do It for Your App

Copy your Working Path into the first column of a simple table. For every step, add the most likely failure and safe next action.

```
STEP
What is the user trying to do?

FAILURE
What could prevent, repeat, corrupt, hide, or reverse the result?

USER MESSAGE
What happened? What can the person do? Is prior work safe?

RECOVERY
Prevent | Retry | Return | Restore | Escalate | Stop safely

PROOF
How will you create the failure and verify the recovery?

OWNER
Product | Founder | Payment provider | Host | Other named party

KNOWN-GOOD CHECKPOINT
Behavior and checks that passed:
Files or version preserved:
How to return:
New data that returning would lose:

AFTER A SUPPORT EVENT
Failure reported:
Time to understand and recover:
Outside provider or cost:
Result:
Change that could prevent a repeat:
```

Keep the plan short. Cover the main path, saved data, and any controlled action inside your Trust Map.

Next, write your support boundary:

```
Support channel:
Realistic response window:
Included help:
Excluded help:
Information we may request:
Refund, replacement, or stop rule:
Owner:
```

If you cannot name an owner, remove the responsibility or stop before launch.

Ask the AI agent to inspect recovery before editing:

```
Review the Working Path, Trust Map, and Recovery Plan.
Do not edit yet.
For each named failure, explain the current behavior, the smallest
safe
recovery, the files involved, and the exact check that would prove
it.
Flag any retry that could repeat a charge, message, deletion,
publication,
or record. Preserve all behavior already proved.
```

Reject vague checks such as "test error handling." Name the starting state, action, expected message, saved state, and final state.

Create a checkpoint. Implement only the approved recovery work. Then run the main path again, because a recovery change can break normal use.

Finally, conduct a recovery drill without the agent guiding each step. Pretend you are the user. Can you understand what happened and return to safety from the interface itself?

If not, the product still depends on the builder being in the room.

Prove It

Your Recovery Plan passes this chapter when:

- each important failure has a safe next action;
- the message matches the product's actual state;
- repeated controlled actions cannot silently repeat;
- a known-good checkpoint and return path exist; and
- support has a real owner and boundary.

Your Result

Save the **Recovery Plan** beside the Trust Map.

You now have a bounded product path another person can try. In Chapter 15, you will turn that product into an offer a buyer can understand.

Chapter 15: Turn the Product Into an Offer

The Move

Sell a result, not a pile of features.

With unQbd, the platform and the offer are different things. Reading, listening, watching, and community describe product capabilities. A membership has to explain which access a specific buyer receives, what it costs, and how that person can begin.

I cannot expect a list of capabilities to make that decision for the buyer.

The offer is that explanation made concrete.

It tells the buyer who the product is for, what result they receive, what is included, what is not included, what help they get, what it costs, and what happens next.

Your result is one **Offer One-Pager**.

Why It Matters

A product is what you built.

An offer is the decision you ask someone to make.

A working product is not yet a complete offer.

The same product can support several offers. A reading platform could be offered to an individual reader, a family, a school, or an organization. Each buyer has a different problem, authority, delivery path, and reason to act.

Trying to speak to all of them at once usually produces weak language such as "for anyone who loves learning."

Return to the buyer you named in Chapter 3.

Begin with the buyer's moment

Describe the moment that makes the buyer look for help.

Not:

> *People need a better productivity experience.*

Better:

> *An adult hobby learner can find the practice plan, but cannot tell which sessions actually happened.*

The second statement gives the buyer a chance to recognize themselves. It also limits the product's responsibility.

State one result

Use the Outcome Promise from Chapter 5.

The result should be visible enough for the buyer to judge. Avoid claims that depend on months of use, perfect behavior, or a feeling you cannot verify.

"Plan one practice session and record what actually happened" is smaller than "master any skill faster."

The smaller claim may sound less dramatic. It is easier to trust, deliver, and improve.

Package the whole experience

The buyer does not receive only the software.

They receive the path around it:

- the way they get access;
- the instructions or setup;
- the product itself;
- the amount of support;
- the time window;
- the data and cancellation path; and
- the result you are willing to stand behind.

A simple app plus a short guided setup may be a stronger first offer than a larger app with no help. The guided setup can show where the buyer gets confused and how much delivery really costs.

Write the limits

Good exclusions make an offer stronger.

They prevent the buyer from assuming that your first version includes coaching, custom development, unlimited support, perfect compatibility, or a result you never promised.

Use direct language:

- works on one supported device;

- no account or cross-device sync;
- support includes two replies during the 14 days after setup;
- does not provide coaching or a curriculum; and
- stores the named data locally in the current browser.

An exclusion should not hide a defect. If the product fails the promised path, fix it. If the buyer expects a different product, state the boundary.

Match help to the uncertainty

Early offers often need more founder involvement because the path is not yet obvious.

That can be useful. You see the buyer's questions instead of guessing. But the help must be measurable.

Replace "personal support" with:

- one 30-minute setup call;
- two support replies;
- one device configuration; or
- a response within two business days during a stated window.

Measured help lets you calculate whether the offer can work as a business.

Use evidence without pretending

Your first offer may not have testimonials, sales, or long-term results. Do not manufacture them.

Use the evidence you actually have:

- the broken moment you observed;
- the current method and why it falls short;
- the working product path;
- the behavior tests you completed;
- the trust and recovery limits; and
- a clear invitation to a bounded first group.

You can say the product is a beta if it is a beta. You can say the offer is a first test. A buyer can still decide when the offer is honest.

Make the next step obvious

Every offer needs one action.

Buy. Request access. Schedule the setup. Join the waitlist. Reply with a specific answer.

Do not place five equal buttons around the decision. Choose the action your current delivery can support.

If you are not ready to collect payment, use an inquiry-first offer and record whether qualified people ask to continue. Do not call interest a sale.

Keep the product and offer separate

This separation protects your decisions.

If people do not buy, the product may not be the problem. The audience, language, price, trust, timing, or buyer path may be wrong.

If people buy but cannot receive the promised result, the offer language is not the main problem. The product or delivery is.

One page that names both sides makes the next test easier to read.

Keep the Offer One-Pager beside the product brief. When either one changes, check the other so the buyer never receives a promise the current product cannot keep.

Test what the buyer believes they bought

The buyer's interpretation matters more than the sentence you intended.

After someone reads the offer, ask them to complete these statements:

```
This is for someone who:
After using it, I expect to:
The price includes:
The price does not include:
If I need help, I can:
My next step would be:
```

Compare the answers with the Offer One-Pager.

If the buyer expects ongoing coaching and you offer two support replies, the offer is unclear. If they expect an account and sync while the product stores data on one device, the product boundary is unclear. If they cannot name the result, more features will not rescue the offer.

Fix the smallest wording or packaging mismatch. Do not add the buyer's imagined feature merely because the offer accidentally implied it.

Run the same check on the final purchase or inquiry screen. A clear sales page can still hand the buyer to a vague action such as `Get Started` with no explanation of what happens next.

The offer passes when the buyer can repeat the same exchange you are prepared to deliver.

Practice Loop

In this constructed offer scenario, Practice Loop is a browser app. It creates one practice plan, records an honest outcome, stores the current plan and recent result locally, and lets the user delete that local data.

The first offer hypothesis is **Practice Loop Guided Setup** for an adult hobby learner.

The offer includes:

- one 30-minute guided setup;
- help entering one practice routine the buyer has chosen;
- configuration on one supported device;
- the public beta app;
- up to two support replies during the 14 days after setup; and

- a written local-data removal path.

It does not include reminders, coaching, a skill curriculum, an account, sync, a teacher dashboard, device transfer, or ongoing support after the stated window.

The guided setup helps the buyer use the app. It does not prescribe what or how to practice. The 30-minute appointment and later support replies are separate parts of the same offer.

The buyer's next step is to purchase the one-time guided setup or use the approved inquiry path if payment is not ready.

The offer does not claim that the app improves skill, guarantees practice, or creates a lasting habit. Its claim stays inside the product evidence:

> *Plan one practice session and record what actually happened.*

Do It for Your App

Write the offer on one page before designing a sales page.

```
OFFER NAME
A plain name the buyer can repeat

FIRST BUYER
The narrow person or organization this is for

BUYER MOMENT
What is happening when they look for help?

RESULT
What specific result will they receive?

PRODUCT
What does the app do to create that result?

INCLUDED
Access, setup, support, delivery, and time window

NOT INCLUDED
Important limits and excluded expectations

EVIDENCE
What can you honestly show or state today?

PRICE HYPOTHESIS
The amount or inquiry step you will test

NEXT ACTION
The one thing the buyer should do
```

Read the page as if you were the buyer.

Can you answer these questions without talking to the founder?

- Is this for me?
- What changes after I use it?
- What exactly do I receive?
- What help will I get?
- What important thing is not included?
- What will I be asked to pay or do?
- What happens immediately after I say yes?

If the page needs a long conversation to explain the basics, the offer is not clear yet.

Ask the AI agent to challenge it without rewriting the truth:

```
Review this Offer One-Pager against the Buyer Map, Outcome Promise,
Working Path, Trust Map, and Recovery Plan.
Identify any claim the evidence does not support, any buyer
expectation the
offer leaves unresolved, and any included support that is not
operationally
defined. Suggest simpler wording. Do not invent proof, urgency,
results,
testimonials, scarcity, or guarantees.
```

Keep the final decision yourself. An AI model may make language sound more persuasive by making the claim broader. Broader is not automatically better.

Now read every included item as an operational promise. If you offer setup, can you schedule it? If you offer replies, who responds? If you promise deletion, does the path work? If access ends, how is that explained?

Remove anything you cannot deliver during the test.

Finally, show the one-page offer to a few relevant people without asking whether they like it. Ask them to explain what they believe they would receive, what result they expect, and what they would do next.

Misunderstanding is evidence. Fix the offer before adding persuasion.

Prove It

Your Offer One-Pager passes this chapter when:

- one buyer can recognize their moment;
- one result matches the product evidence;
- included help has a real amount and owner;
- important exclusions are visible; and
- one price or inquiry action leads to a clear next step.

Your Result

Save the **Offer One-Pager**.

In Chapter 16, you will choose a price hypothesis and make sure the buyer can travel from the offer to the promised delivery.

Chapter 16: Set the Price and Complete the Buyer Path

The Move

Choose one test price and walk the whole buyer path.

Price is important. It is not the whole business.

A person can understand the offer and still fail to buy because the payment path is confusing. They can pay and never receive the setup instructions. They can receive access and not know where to begin. They can need help and find no support path.

That fragmentation is one reason I kept returning to the original unQbd idea. Separate pieces can each work while the person's overall experience still fails.

Treat the buyer path as one product.

Your result is one **Buyer Path** with a price hypothesis.

Why It Matters

The buyer path begins before payment and ends after delivery.

Use six handoffs:

1. **Discover:** the right person encounters the offer.
2. **Understand:** they can tell whether it is for them and what it does.
3. **Decide:** they see the price, limits, and next action.
4. **Complete:** payment or inquiry works and produces a clear confirmation.
5. **Receive:** access, setup, or delivery arrives as promised.
6. **Use and recover:** they can begin, get help, and remove their data or end the relationship.

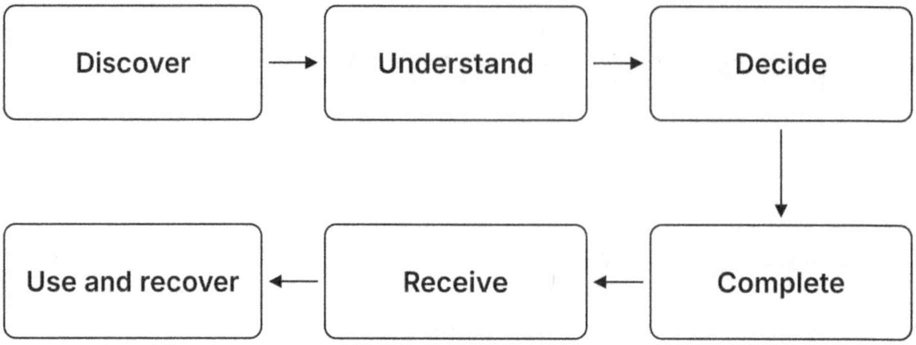

Every handoff must agree with the promise.

A failure at any handoff can look like weak demand. That is why you record the path, not only the purchase count.

Walk the path in order. A polished checkout cannot repair an unclear offer, and a clear offer cannot repair delivery that never arrives.

Write one owner beside every handoff before testing it.

Treat price as a hypothesis

You do not discover the perfect price in a spreadsheet.

Choose a price that fits the buyer, promised result, delivery effort, risk, and alternative. Then test it without changing it after every reaction.

Ask four questions:

- Is the amount believable for the result?
- Can the intended buyer approve it?
- Can you deliver the offer without losing money or time you cannot sustain?
- Is the price simple enough to explain in one line?

Your first test price can be wrong. Its job is to create evidence.

Count the whole delivery cost

Software may feel free after it is built. The offer is not free to deliver.

Include:

- transaction costs;
- your setup or support time;
- hosting or service use;
- refunds or replacements you expect to own;
- fixed launch work; and
- any required tax, compliance, or professional cost you have actually verified.

Keep assumptions labeled. A payment provider's current fee, eligibility rule, and tax feature can change. Verify the real terms before publication instead of copying an old number from a book.

For an early test, use a simple planning rate for your time. It is not a salary claim. It makes labor visible.

The basic calculation is:

> ***Contribution per sale = Price - Variable cash costs - Delivery time cost***

Count each cost once. Keep setup and support labor out of variable cash costs if you subtract that labor separately.

Fixed launch work is separate. If contribution is positive, you can estimate how many sales would recover the fixed cost. If it is negative, more sales make the problem larger.

Do not build card handling

Use an approved hosted checkout from a reputable payment provider when the offer is ready and you are eligible to use it.

The provider should handle sensitive card entry. Payment secrets do not belong in a public browser project, source file, prompt, screenshot, or chat transcript.

Before live use, verify the provider's current:

- account and age eligibility;
- fees and payout timing;
- refund and dispute controls;
- tax settings and responsibilities;
- confirmation and delivery behavior; and
- terms for your product and location.

If those items are not ready, use an inquiry-first path. A request to buy is useful evidence, but it is not revenue.

For a reader under 18, an adult must own the payment account, approve the offer, and control live financial activity.

Test both success and failure

The buyer needs a clear answer after every attempt.

Verify payment in the provider's authoritative record. For a small manual offer, that can be the provider's dashboard. Match the buyer, amount, offer, live or test mode, and payment status. A return page or a buyer's screenshot is not payment proof.

Treat pending payment as pending. Do not deliver based on an unconfirmed return screen or ask the buyer to pay again before checking the first attempt.

On success:

- show that the action completed;
- send or display a receipt through the approved provider;
- explain what arrives next and when;
- provide the first use step; and
- name the support path.

On failure or cancellation:

- do not claim payment completed;
- do not deliver paid access by accident;
- let the buyer safely retry or leave; and

- preserve enough information to help without exposing sensitive data.

Use test mode or the provider's approved testing method. Do not run repeated real charges merely to see what happens.

Keep delivery simple at first

Automation can wait until the path is understood.

For the first few buyers, manual confirmation and scheduling may be responsible. You can see where handoffs fail and record the actual time.

Manual does not mean improvised. Write the steps:

1. confirm the approved payment or inquiry;
2. send the promised instruction;
3. schedule or deliver the setup;
4. provide the stated access;
5. record support time; and
6. close the loop with the buyer.

Do not automate a path you have not successfully delivered by hand.

Track where people stop

Do not collapse the buyer path into bought or did not buy.

Record:

- eligible people;
- people reached;
- replies;
- qualified decisions;
- payment attempts;
- completed purchases;
- completed deliveries; and
- initial use.

Each count answers a different question. Ten people reached with no replies is different from five replies and five objections. A purchase with failed delivery is not a successful path.

The counts can stay small. Clear evidence is more useful than impressive-looking traffic.

Earn the public route

An app can work locally and still be unready for a public address.

If the offer requires public access, treat hosting as another handoff. Decide who owns the host, what information crosses the boundary, whether logs or analytics are active, how you identify the known-good version, and how you remove or restore it.

Ask the agent to prepare a separate publish folder containing only the files the public app needs. Keep briefs, research notes, build logs, backups, private records, and credentials out of it. Review the file list before uploading. Your whole project folder is not the public product.

Ask the AI agent to prepare the smallest publish plan and test it through an approved preview. The account owner approves the live action. After publication, run the main path, disclosure, deletion, failure, and recovery checks again at the real address.

A live link proves availability. It does not prove demand.

Keep cash, labor, and fixed work separate

One total can hide three different business questions.

Cash per sale is the money received minus transaction, service, refund, and other per-sale cash costs.

Contribution after labor also subtracts the value you assigned to setup and support time.

Result after fixed work then subtracts one-time launch, design, review, or setup cost.

Show all three when they matter:

```
Cash after variable cash cost:
Contribution after delivery labor:
Result after fixed test cost:
```

A sale can bring in positive cash while requiring too much founder time. A test can show negative results after fixed work while each additional responsible sale still contributes positively. Those situations need different decisions.

Do not erase fixed work to make the first launch look profitable. Do not subtract the same fixed work from every future sale. Keep the units visible so the scorecard can read the business honestly.

The price is a buyer decision. The cost model is a founder decision. Both must work for the offer to continue.

Practice Loop

In this constructed pricing scenario, Practice Loop tests a one-time price of **$49** for Guided Setup.

The scenario uses these planning assumptions:

Item	Scenario amount
Price	$49.00
Transaction cost placeholder	$2.00
45 minutes of delivery and support at a $30 per hour internal planning rate	$22.50
Hosting allocation	$0.50
Contribution before fixed launch cost	$24.00
Fixed launch setup cost	$120.00

At $24 contribution per sale, the scenario needs five sales to recover the $120 fixed launch cost.

Every number is hypothetical. The transaction cost is not a provider quote. Taxes, refunds, disputes, and other obligations remain unverified and excluded. A real builder must replace the assumptions with current evidence.

Before the offer test, the constructed case publishes a static version through an approved maintained host. The app adds no account or analytics, sends no user-entered practice data to a server, and continues to keep the current plan in that browser. The builder verifies the disclosure, deletion control, main path, recovery path, and known-good return at the public address.

The host still receives requests to load the app and may keep access logs. The local-only claim covers the entered practice data, not every piece of connection information. The public address starts with its own empty storage. The builder also rechecks offline behavior; local testing did not prove that the public page will reload without a connection.

The public beta app remains usable without an account. The paid offer is guided setup and bounded support, not secret access to the public page.

The path uses an approved hosted payment page or an approved inquiry-first fallback. After confirmation, the founder manually schedules the setup, provides the stated support, and records the time.

The test keeps the offer, scope, and $49 price unchanged through one bounded launch to at most 12 eligible known adult hobby learners.

Do It for Your App

First, write your price card.

```
TEST PRICE
One amount or one inquiry action

BUYER
Who can approve and pay?

VALUE REASON
Why could the result justify this amount?

VARIABLE CASH COSTS
Transaction, service, refund, and other per-sale cash costs

DELIVERY LABOR
Preparation, setup, support, and follow-up time at the stated
planning rate

FIXED TEST COST
One-time setup, design, review, or launch work

UNVERIFIED ITEMS
Fees, tax, eligibility, refunds, or terms still requiring current
evidence

TEST CUTOFF
Maximum qualified contacts and the response deadline
Maximum buyers you can serve and the support measurement window
```

Then map the six handoffs from discovery through recovery.

For each handoff, name:

- the buyer's action;
- the screen, message, or person responsible;
- the evidence that proves completion;
- the likely failure; and
- the safe recovery.

Do not use a successful test payment as proof of the entire path. Continue until the buyer receives the promised access or setup and can begin.

Ask the AI agent for a path review:

```
Review the Offer One-Pager, price card, Trust Map, Recovery Plan,
and proposed
Buyer Path. Do not publish, charge, message, or change a live
account.
Identify missing handoffs, unsupported claims, sensitive
information in the
wrong place, repeated-action risks, and any delivery step without
an owner.
Return a test plan for success, cancellation, failure,
confirmation, delivery,
support, and removal.
```

Use provider test mode only after the account owner approves the specific setup. Keep credentials out of prompts and source files. Stop if the tool asks to handle card data directly.

Run the path yourself. Then ask another person to explain what they believe will happen before and after the decision. Confusion before a live launch is cheap evidence.

Record the first real delivery time separately from your estimate. A 30-minute call plus 25 minutes of messages is 55 minutes of delivery and support, not 30.

Set both a contact limit and a response deadline. Leave the price unchanged through that test unless the path is unsafe or the offer cannot be delivered. If too few people decide, record the missing evidence at the deadline. Do not keep extending the test until the result looks better.

Prove It

Your Buyer Path passes this chapter when:

- one test price has labeled cost assumptions;
- every handoff has an action, owner, proof, and recovery;
- sensitive payment handling stays with an approved provider;
- confirmation leads to the promised delivery and first use; and
- the test cutoff is set before launch.

Your Result

Save the **Buyer Path** and price card.

In Chapter 17, you will choose the first small audience that can actually recognize, approve, and receive the offer.

Part V: Launch, Learn, and Decide

Chapter 17: Choose the First Audience

The Move

Choose the smallest audience that can recognize and act on the offer.

At unQbd, a technical-book reader, a parent choosing a children's product, and a general fiction reader can all recognize the company. That does not make them one buying audience.

If I am offering a technical book, the first audience needs that topic. If I am offering a family product, the parent needs to recognize the value and control the decision.

The company name can stay the same. The person, reason to act, and path to the offer still need to match.

Use the same discipline for your app. Your product may eventually help many people. Your first offer still needs a reachable group.

Your result is one **Audience List**.

Why It Matters

"Everyone" is not an audience you can test.

It does not tell you where to find people, what language they recognize, who can approve the purchase, or why the offer matters now.

A first audience is not the permanent limit of the company. It is the group from whom you can collect the cleanest next evidence.

Use three audience tests

A useful first audience is:

1. **Eligible:** the offer truly fits their problem, situation, and requirements.
2. **Reachable:** you have an appropriate way to contact or appear in front of them.

3. **Able to act:** the person can decide, pay, obtain approval, or take the next step.

A group can pass two tests and still fail the third.

Teen app builders may be eligible for a course and reachable through a school. They may not own the payment decision. The parent, school, or program may be the buyer or approver.

Adult hobby learners may recognize the constructed Practice Loop offer and control a $49 purchase. If you have no appropriate way to reach them, they are not a practical first audience yet.

Start from the Buyer Map

Return to Chapter 3. Name the user, buyer, and approver separately.

For a direct consumer app, one person may hold all three roles. For a school, family, company, or youth program, the roles can split.

Your audience language should match the person who sees it.

A user message says:

> *Plan one practice session and record what actually happened.*

A buyer message may say:

> *Guided setup helps an adult hobby learner begin using the simple planning loop on one supported device.*

An approver may need to understand price, privacy, time, safety, and support before caring about feature details.

Do not ask one paragraph to speak equally to all three people.

Choose a qualifying signal

An audience label is not enough.

"Musicians" can include professionals, teachers, parents, students, hobbyists, performers, and people who no longer practice.

Add a behavior or situation that makes the offer relevant:

- has chosen a hobby they practice at least occasionally;
- can find practice intentions but cannot tell what actually happened;
- uses a supported browser and device;
- wants a simple planning step rather than coaching; and
- can make or approve the buying decision.

These qualifications keep your launch count honest. A person is not an eligible contact merely because you can find their email address.

Begin with a warm, appropriate path

The first launch does not require a giant following.

It requires a legitimate path to a small number of relevant people.

That path may be:

- people you already know who match the criteria;
- a community where the offer is allowed and relevant;
- a partner who serves the audience and agrees to share it;
- a small existing customer or reader list with the right permission; or
- direct conversations created through your earlier problem research.

Do not scrape a list, pretend a cold contact is warm, or use a private community against its rules. Reachability includes permission and context.

Make the count small enough to read

A bounded first audience protects the experiment.

Choose enough qualified decisions to reveal basic patterns, but few enough that you can deliver the offer yourself and inspect every handoff.

Ten or twelve people may be more useful than a public post seen by thousands if you can answer:

- who was eligible;
- who actually received the offer;

- who replied;
- what decision they made;
- whether the buyer path worked; and
- how much support delivery required.

A view count cannot answer those questions by itself.

Do not confuse followers with buyers

Your existing audience may know you for something else.

Someone who follows a children's reading product may not be the buyer for an AI app-building course. A software reader may not be looking for a family membership. An audience can trust the founder and still be wrong for the offer.

Use relevance before reach.

This is especially important when one company serves more than one kind of customer. Keep the offer attached to the audience that can act on it.

Write the exclusion line

Every first audience needs a visible outside edge.

For example:

> *This first test is for adult hobby learners using one supported device. It is not for instructors managing students, people who need cross-device sync, or anyone seeking skill coaching.*

That line keeps friendly but unqualified interest from changing the product during the test.

It also lets you record an honest no-fit reason instead of treating every nonbuyer as rejection.

Protect younger participants

If the user is under 18, the live business path changes.

An adult should approve outreach, account ownership, payment, public posting, data collection, and direct contact. School or program rules may add another approval layer.

The student can still build, observe, and learn. They should not be asked to create live financial or privacy risk merely to complete the method.

Your book or product can have a general audience while a youth program uses a bounded adult-owned path.

Separate the audience from the channel

The audience is who should receive the offer. The channel is how the offer reaches them.

Do not let the channel choose the person.

If you have a large following on one platform, it can be tempting to define the audience as whoever follows you there. The followers may know you for another topic, lack buying authority, or never experience the broken moment.

Write the two decisions separately:

```
Audience:
Why the offer fits:

Channel:
Why the audience appropriately uses or trusts this path:
Permission or rule that applies:
```

One audience can be tested through several channels. One channel can contain several unrelated audiences. Keep the evidence attached to the exact combination.

If direct conversations produce decisions and a public post produces only views, do not combine them into one conversion rate. The context and action were different.

A weak channel does not prove a weak problem. A large channel does not prove a strong buyer fit. The Launch Log should let you tell them apart.

Name the source beside every contact. That keeps referrals, research conversations, community posts, and existing customers from becoming one misleading audience total.

Practice Loop

Practice Loop chooses a constructed first audience of 12 known adult hobby learners.

Each person must:

- practice a self-chosen hobby at least occasionally;
- recognize the gap between a visible practice plan and its missing outcome;
- use the supported browser and one device;
- want planning and honest recording rather than coaching; and
- control their own $49 purchase decision.

The audience excludes instructors seeking a student dashboard, people who require reminders or sync, and anyone asking for performance guarantees.

The founder has an appropriate individual contact path to each person. The launch will not use a scraped list, bulk message, public income claim, or manufactured urgency.

Twelve is the contact limit, not a required number of decisions or a demand forecast. The constructed test allows seven days for responses after the last invitation. The founder then records who was reached, who decided, and what remains unknown. Silence does not extend the cutoff.

Do It for Your App

Build the Audience List from your Buyer Map and Offer One-Pager.

```
FIRST AUDIENCE
One narrow group

QUALIFYING MOMENT
What must be happening for the offer to matter now?

ELIGIBLE
What makes the person a real fit?

REACHABLE
What appropriate path can place the offer in front of them?

ABLE TO ACT
Who can decide, approve, pay, and receive delivery?

EXCLUDED
Who is close to the audience but outside this test?

COUNT
Maximum qualified contacts, response deadline, and delivery
capacity
```

Now list specific people or organizations only when you have a legitimate reason to believe they fit. Do not put private contact information into a public prompt. Use initials or a local record if the AI agent does not need the identity.

For each entry, mark:

- eligibility known, likely, or unknown;
- contact path permitted or unverified;
- decision authority yes, no, or unknown; and
- reason the offer may matter now.

Unknown is not failure. It tells you what to verify before outreach.

Ask the AI agent to review the audience definition, not to scrape contacts:

```
Compare the Audience List with the Buyer Map, Offer One-Pager,
price, delivery
limits, and Trust Map. Identify weak qualifications, role
confusion, people
who cannot approve the action, and exclusions that should be
explicit.
Do not search for, enrich, scrape, or message any person. Do not
infer private
traits. Return only improvements to the audience definition and
launch count.
```

Choose a count your current delivery can handle. If every buyer requires 45 minutes of setup and support, twelve buyers require nine hours, plus outreach and any overruns. Your capacity belongs in the audience decision.

Finally, write one sentence for the audience and one sentence for the outside edge.

If a person does not fit, do not persuade them harder. Record no fit and protect the test.

Prove It

Your Audience List passes this chapter when:

- eligibility depends on a real behavior or situation;
- an appropriate reach path exists;
- the user, buyer, and approver can act;
- exclusions protect the offer boundary; and
- the launch count fits your delivery capacity.

Your Result

Save the **Audience List** with the Offer One-Pager.

In Chapter 18, you will make one clear invitation, deliver what was promised, and record what actually happened.

Chapter 18: Make the Offer and Launch

The Move

Ask the first audience to make a real decision.

Publishing a page is not the same as launching an offer.

The page can be live while no qualified person sees it. People can see it and not understand the next step. They can reply politely without deciding. They can buy and never receive the result.

I have to separate those moments in every unQbd launch. Product availability, audience reach, buyer action, delivery, and use are different facts.

Your first launch can be small. It cannot be vague.

Your result is one **Launch Log**.

Why It Matters

Until someone faces the offer, most business questions remain guesses.

A response can be a purchase, an explicit no, not now, no fit, or a question that leaves the decision open. Keep those outcomes separate. A useful question is evidence, but it is not yet a buying decision.

The launch turns the offer into evidence by controlling three things:

1. who receives it;
2. what they are asked to do; and
3. what you record without changing the rules halfway through.

Use one clear invitation

The invitation should let a qualified person decide without a sales puzzle.

It needs:

- the buyer moment;
- the narrow result;
- what is included;
- the important limit;
- the price or inquiry step;
- the next action; and
- the honest reason for the bounded first test.

A constructed Practice Loop invitation reads:

> *I am testing a guided setup for adult hobby learners whose practice notes show the plan but not what happened. The $49 one-time offer includes a 30-minute setup on one supported device, the Practice Loop beta, and two support replies during the 14 days after setup. It does not include coaching, reminders, or cross-device sync. Would you like to see the full offer and decide whether it fits?*

The first sentence does not need hype. It needs recognition.

Ask for a decision, not encouragement

Friends and early supporters often want to be kind.

Questions such as "Do you like this?" or "Would you use this someday?" make kindness easy and evidence weak.

Ask for the next real action:

- Would you like to buy the guided setup at $49?
- Would you like the approved payment or inquiry link?
- Is this a no, not now, or a question you need answered before deciding?

Do not pressure the person. Clear options make a respectful no easier.

A no can protect you from building the wrong thing. An unclear maybe can keep you busy for months.

Keep the offer stable through the cutoff

The first objection will tempt you to change the price. The first feature request will tempt you to change the product. The first silence will tempt you to change the audience.

Record before changing.

Keep the audience criteria, core offer, price, and delivery boundary stable until the cutoff from Chapters 16 and 17. Stop early only if you discover a trust problem, false claim, broken buyer path, or offer you cannot deliver.

Without that stability, ten conversations become ten different tests.

Record the launch in stages

Use separate counts:

- **Eligible:** met the audience criteria.
- **Reached:** the invitation actually arrived through an appropriate path.
- **Replied:** gave any response.
- **Decided:** made an explicit yes or no decision on the offer. Keep deferred and unresolved replies separate.
- **Purchased:** completed approved payment.
- **Delivered:** received what the offer promised.
- **Used:** completed the first meaningful product action.

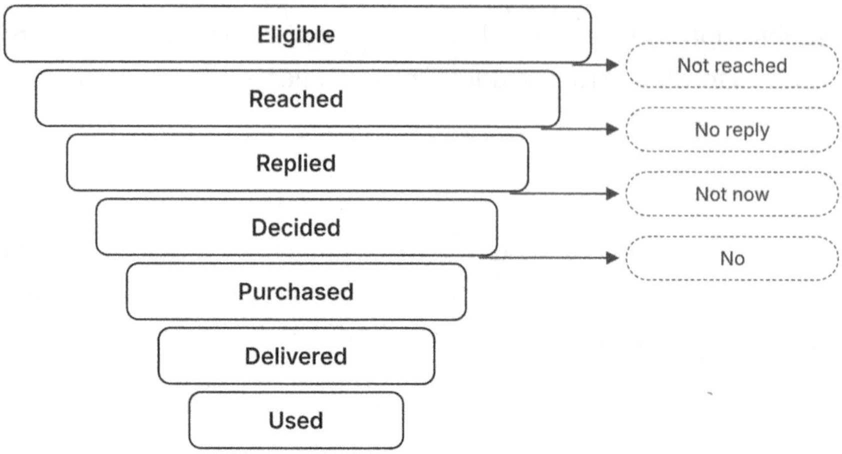

A launch is a chain of counted events.

Do not turn a reply into a qualified decision. Do not turn a payment attempt into revenue. Do not turn access into use.

One person can appear in several stages, but only once in each count. Keep side outcomes visible too. Not reached, no reply, no fit, no, and not now describe different breaks in the path. Combining them into one lost group destroys the evidence you need for the next decision.

Record words without inventing meaning

When a person explains a decision, capture a short accurate note.

Separate:

- what they said;
- what they did;
- what you think it may mean; and
- what next evidence would test that interpretation.

"Too expensive" may mean the amount is wrong. It may also mean the result is unclear, the person is not the buyer, the timing is wrong, or the offer is not important enough.

One comment does not choose the answer.

Deliver before celebrating

A purchase creates an obligation.

Follow the Buyer Path. Confirm the transaction through the approved system. Send the promised instruction. Complete the setup. Provide access. Record support time. Verify that the buyer can begin.

Do not announce success while the buyer is still waiting for delivery.

If the path fails, recover according to Chapter 14. That may mean retrying, helping manually, refunding through the approved provider, or stopping the launch until the failure is fixed.

Observe use with permission

Initial use is different from purchase.

Use only the evidence method the buyer understands and accepts. For a small manual offer, you can ask at a stated time whether they completed the key action. You do not need hidden tracking.

Ask about behavior:

- Did you create the first result?
- Where did you stop?
- What required help?
- What did you expect to happen?

Do not claim retention from a few days of use. Record the time window.

Keep outreach responsible

Send only through appropriate channels. Respect community rules, consent, privacy, and requests to stop.

Do not use the AI agent to mass-message people merely because it can. Do not let it send live outreach, change a payment account, publish the offer, or spend money without the account owner's explicit approval.

For a youth-led project, an adult owns those live actions and direct buyer communications.

Use dates and states, not memory

A launch develops over time.

Someone may receive the invitation on Monday, reply on Wednesday, ask a question on Friday, and decide the next week. If you record only the final word, you lose the path and time required.

For each important change, record:

```
Date:
Prior state:
New state:
Evidence source:
Next action owed:
Owner:
```

Do not overwrite `question` with `purchase` and pretend the buyer moved directly from reached to paid. Preserve the state changes.

This also prevents an old intention from looking current. A person who says "send me the link next month" has not purchased and may not belong in the current cutoff. Record the future action without moving the current result.

Close the operational loop

At the end of each launch day, review obligations before totals.

Ask:

- Is any buyer waiting for confirmation or delivery?
- Does any person expect an answer?
- Did a failed action create a retry, refund, or recovery obligation?
- Did anyone ask not to be contacted again?
- Did the offer create support work outside the written boundary?

Resolve or assign those items before sending more invitations.

A bounded launch can stop before the planned count when delivery begins to fail. Capacity is a trust boundary. The next contact should not become a buyer you cannot serve because the log says three invitations remain.

Practice Loop

Practice Loop makes the same constructed offer to 12 eligible known adult hobby learners.

The invitation cycle ends at the contact limit and the seven-day response deadline from Chapter 17. The counts below are frozen at that cutoff. Delivery and the promised support continue afterward when needed.

The Launch Log records:

Result	Count
Eligible contacts	12
Reached	10
Not reached	2
Replies	5
No reply	5
Purchase	1
Explicit no	1
Undecided or question without decision	3

The one constructed buyer pays $49 and completes the guided setup. Across setup and the full 14-day support window, delivery and support total 55 minutes rather than the planned 45. The case closes that measurement only after the promised support window ends.

During the first seven days after setup, the buyer reports creating four plans and recording three outcomes. That information comes from a voluntary day-seven follow-up, not hidden analytics. It shows initial use during one week. It does not prove retention, improvement, or broad demand.

The other results also remain narrow. Five no replies are not five rejections. One purchase proves one person paid in this case, not that a market has been established.

The five replies contain two completed decisions: one purchase and one explicit no. The other three remain open at the cutoff. Delivery is complete for one buyer, and that buyer reports initial use. Neither count comes from the reply total alone.

Do It for Your App

Prepare the launch before sending or publishing anything.

Write the invitation, audience cutoff, Buyer Path, delivery checklist, support owner, and stop conditions. Verify any current payment, platform, tax, privacy, or eligibility requirement that applies.

Then create the Launch Log:

```
PERSON OR ACCOUNT ID
Use the minimum identifying information needed

QUALIFIED
Yes | No | Unknown, with reason

REACHED
Date, channel, permitted context, and evidence of delivery
If delivery cannot be verified, record sent with reach unknown

RESPONSE
Exact decision or concise accurate note

PAYMENT OR INQUIRY
Attempted | Completed | Failed | Not applicable

DELIVERY
What was delivered, when, and by whom?

INITIAL USE
What first meaningful action occurred, over what time window?

TIME AND COST
Setup, support, service, refund, or other actual amount
Support window still open or complete, with closing date
```

Keep private contact and payment information out of public files and unnecessary AI context.

Before launch, ask the AI agent for a read-only check:

```
Review the final invitation, Audience List, Offer One-Pager, Buyer
Path,
Trust Map, Recovery Plan, delivery checklist, and Launch Log
fields.
Do not publish, send, charge, enroll, or change a live account.
Identify unsupported claims, missing disclosures, unclear
decisions, delivery
gaps, privacy risks, and stop conditions that are not operational.
```

Fix real problems. Preserve the approved offer through the cutoff.

When the account owner is ready, make one authorized launch action at a time. Confirm the visible result. For individual invitations, distinguish sent from verified delivery. If the channel provides no reliable delivery evidence, leave reach unknown. Even verified delivery does not prove the person read the offer.

During delivery, use a timer. Record all setup and support work, including preparation and follow-up. The business cannot learn from invisible labor.

At the cutoff, stop the outreach cycle. Do not start explaining the result from memory. Use the Launch Log.

Freeze a copy before analysis. If a later reply arrives, add a dated update instead of changing the original cutoff result. That preserves the exact evidence behind the decision.

Keep recording delivery and support owed to existing buyers. If a support window is still open, its cost is provisional. Closing outreach does not close the obligations the offer created.

Prove It

Your Launch Log passes this chapter when:

- the same audience, offer, price, and cutoff controlled the test;
- reached, replied, decided, purchased, delivered, and used stay separate;
- each buyer received the promised path or an honest recovery;
- actual time and cost were recorded; and
- every claim remains inside the evidence window.

Your Result

Save the **Launch Log** without rewriting weak results.

In Chapter 19, you will read the product, offer, buyer path, and economics separately so one number does not tell the whole story.

Chapter 19: Read the Business Honestly

The Move

Separate the evidence before you explain the business.

One number can dominate a founder's thinking.

A sale feels like proof. A rejection feels like failure. A large view count feels like attention. A support problem feels like a product problem.

None of those facts should carry the whole decision.

The scorecard should direct the next test. It should not reward the founder for finding the most flattering number in the launch.

When I evaluate an unQbd product or offer, I need to know which part of the system produced the result. I separate whether the right person saw it, the offer made sense, the path worked, the product delivered, and the economics survived delivery.

Read those questions in separate lanes.

Your result is one **Business Scorecard**.

Why It Matters

The goal of a small launch is not to declare victory or defeat.

The goal is to find the current constraint.

Use five evidence lanes:

1. **Problem:** does the broken moment appear real and important for the intended person?
2. **Product:** can the user create the Outcome Promise through the Working Path?

3. **Offer:** does the buyer understand and choose the packaged result at the test price?
4. **Path:** can the person move from discovery through payment, delivery, use, and recovery?
5. **Economics:** does each sale leave enough contribution for the business to continue?

Problem: is the broken moment real and important?

Product: can the user create the promised result?

Offer: does the buyer understand and choose it?

Path: can the person move through payment, delivery, use, and recovery?

Economics: does each sale leave enough contribution to continue?

Read each lane before combining the story.

An unknown in one lane should stay unknown. Do not borrow confidence from another lane.

Read counts as stages

Start with the Launch Log.

For each stage, calculate a rate only when the denominator means something.

- **Reach rate = Reached / Eligible**
- **Reply rate = Replies / Reached**
- **Purchase rate = Purchases / Reached or qualified decisions**
- **Delivery rate = Completed deliveries / Purchases**
- **Initial-use rate = Buyers completing the first action / Delivered buyers**

Label the denominator. One purchase out of ten reached tells a different story from one purchase out of two qualified decisions.

With small numbers, the rate can swing dramatically because of one person. Keep the count beside the percentage. "One of ten" is harder to exaggerate than "10 percent conversion."

Compare rates only when the audience, offer, channel, and cutoff are close enough to make the comparison useful. A warm introduction and a public post may produce different behavior for reasons the percentage cannot explain.

Give silence the right meaning

No reply means no reply.

It does not automatically mean the problem is weak, the price is high, or the person rejected you. The person may not have read the delivered message, the timing may be poor, or the offer may not matter enough to answer. If delivery itself is unknown, keep that separate too.

Silence can still be useful. Repeated silence among clearly eligible people may show that the invitation, channel, urgency, or problem is weak. It needs another bounded test, not a confident story.

Read objections by lane

Place each objection where it belongs.

What you hear or observe	Possible lane
"I do not have this problem"	Problem or audience
"I do not understand what I get"	Offer
"I cannot approve the purchase"	Buyer or path
Payment or confirmation fails	Path
User cannot create the promised result	Product
Setup consumes too much time	Economics or product

The word possible matters. An objection is a clue, not an automatic diagnosis.

Recalculate with actual labor

Return to the price card from Chapter 16. Replace planning assumptions with the launch actuals.

> *Actual contribution per sale = Price - Actual variable fees - Actual delivery time cost - Other per-sale cost*

Then compare actual contribution with fixed test cost.

Fixed cost does not make a positive sale unprofitable forever. It tells you how many similar contributions would be required to recover the launch investment.

If the actual contribution shrinks because support takes longer than planned, do not hide the time. The business either needs a higher price, simpler delivery, lower support, better onboarding, or a different offer.

Separate use from outcome

A buyer can use the product without receiving a long-term benefit.

Creating four plans is usage. Recording three results is completion behavior. Becoming a better musician, building a habit, or continuing for six months would require different evidence.

Name the exact behavior and window you observed.

This protects the customer and the business. You can improve what actually happened instead of marketing a result you hope will happen later.

Read counterevidence

Counterevidence is information that weakens the story you want to tell.

Examples include:

- relevant people using an existing method successfully;
- a buyer misunderstanding the main result;
- a working product that still requires founder rescue;
- delivery time exceeding the price model;
- people asking for a different offer; or

- initial use that stops immediately.

Write it beside supporting evidence. A scorecard that contains only positive facts is marketing copy, not a decision tool.

Use confidence labels

For each lane, choose one label:

- **Supported for this test:** the bounded evidence directly supports the statement.
- **Mixed:** supporting and counterevidence both matter.
- **Unknown:** the test did not answer the question.
- **Contradicted:** the observed result conflicts with the current claim or model.

Do not use proven for a broad market claim after a tiny test.

The label controls the next experiment. Unknown calls for evidence. Contradicted calls for a change or stop. Supported for this test allows the current piece to stay while another constraint is tested.

Build a denominator tree

Rates become clearer when you draw the audience as a sequence rather than a pile of percentages.

```
Eligible
  Reached
    Replied
      Made a qualified decision
        Purchased
          Received delivery
            Completed first use
```

Write the count at every line for an invitation-led path that actually uses these stages. A buyer may pay directly without sending a separate reply. Record that real route instead of inventing an earlier message to make the tree fit.

For the constructed case, the tree is 12 eligible, 10 reached, 5 replies, 2 completed decisions, 1 purchase, 1 completed delivery, and 1 reported initial use. The three unresolved replies stay outside the completed-decision count.

Now ask where the largest meaningful drop occurs. Ten eligible people with only three reached points toward the channel or contact path. Ten reached with no replies points toward the invitation, timing, channel, or problem. Purchases with failed delivery point toward operations, not demand.

The tree does not diagnose the cause by itself. It shows where the cause probably lives.

Keep unknowns beside the constraint

Choosing one constraint does not make every other question answered.

Write:

- current constraint;
- evidence supporting it;
- important unknowns not controlling this test; and
- what would cause you to replace the constraint.

This keeps focus without manufacturing certainty.

In the constructed Practice Loop case, delivery time can be the current constraint while buyer demand remains unknown. The next bounded test can target onboarding because that is the clearest observed weakness. If qualified offers then produce no purchases, the offer evidence may become the next constraint.

The scorecard is allowed to change its mind when new evidence changes the system.

Practice Loop

The constructed Practice Loop launch records one $49 purchase from ten reached adult hobby learners. Five people reply. One says no. Three remain undecided or ask a question without making a decision.

The buyer completes setup and reports four plans with three recorded outcomes during seven days. Delivery and support across the full 14-day support window take 55 minutes rather than the planned 45. The usage window and cost window measure different things.

The actual scenario economics are:

Item	Scenario result
Revenue	$49.00
Transaction cost placeholder	$2.00
55 minutes at the $30 per hour planning rate	$27.50
Hosting allocation	$0.50
Contribution before fixed launch cost	$19.00
Fixed launch setup cost	$120.00
Result after fixed launch cost	-$101.00
Break-even count at observed contribution	7 sales

The calculation is $49 - $2 - $27.50 - $0.50 = $19. After the $120 fixed cost, the result is -$101. Recovering $120 at $19 per sale requires rounding 6.32 up to seven sales in total, including the first sale.

This is a scenario calculation using placeholder fees and the stated value of labor. It excludes the unverified obligations listed in Chapter 16. Seven sales is not a forecast or a claim of full business profitability.

The scorecard reads the lanes separately:

- **Problem: mixed.** Earlier evidence showed repeated gaps for some adults and working alternatives for others.
- **Product: supported for this test.** One buyer created plans and recorded outcomes during seven days. Retention and skill improvement remain unknown.
- **Offer: unknown.** One purchase proves one buyer paid. The sample is too small to establish demand at $49.
- **Path: supported with friction.** Purchase and delivery completed, but support exceeded the plan.
- **Economics: contradicted at the planned delivery budget.** Contribution remained positive, but actual labor reduced it from $24 to $19 and raised scenario break-even from five sales to seven.

The current constraint is delivery time. Feature requests for reminders or sync do not outrank that evidence.

Do It for Your App

Create one row for each evidence lane.

```
LANE
Problem | Product | Offer | Path | Economics

SUPPORTING EVIDENCE
Counts, behavior, payment, delivery, time, or direct decision

COUNTEREVIDENCE
What weakens the current story?

LIMIT
What did this test not measure?

LABEL
Supported for this test | Mixed | Unknown | Contradicted

NEXT QUESTION
What one question would reduce the most important uncertainty?
```

Use the actual Launch Log. Keep counts beside rates. Replace estimated labor with recorded time. Mark unverified provider fees or obligations instead of treating a placeholder as fact.

Ask the AI agent to check the arithmetic and challenge the interpretation:

```
Using only the supplied Launch Log, price card, delivery records,
and product
evidence, calculate each rate and contribution. Show the
denominator and
formula. Separate observed fact, arithmetic, founder
interpretation, and
unknown. Identify any claim that exceeds the sample or time window.
Do not invent missing values or recommend a feature yet.
```

Verify every input before accepting the output. AI can calculate correctly from the wrong number.

Then write one sentence for the current constraint:

> *The next decision is most limited by* ____________ *because* ____________.

Choose one constraint. Other unknowns can remain visible without controlling the next experiment.

If the product does not deliver the promise, product is likely the constraint. If qualified people understand but refuse the offer, offer or price may be the constraint. If people buy but delivery consumes the margin, economics or onboarding may be the constraint.

Do not choose the feature that sounds most exciting. Choose the constraint supported by the scorecard.

Prove It

Your Business Scorecard passes this chapter when:

- problem, product, offer, path, and economics stay separate;
- counts, rates, denominators, and time windows are visible;
- actual labor replaces the delivery estimate;
- counterevidence and unknowns remain on the page; and
- one current constraint follows from the evidence.

Your Result

Save the **Business Scorecard** and current constraint.

In Chapter 20, you will use that constraint to continue one bounded experiment, change the offer, or stop responsibly.

Chapter 20: Decide What Happens Next

The Move

Make one founder decision from the evidence.

The app is not the final result of this book.

The final result is the ability to decide what the app and business deserve next.

AI makes continuing easy. You can always ask for another screen, feature, redesign, channel, or campaign. That speed can hide a weak decision.

I have had to keep returning to this distinction with unQbd. The vision can remain broad while the next move stays narrow. I do not need to build every part of the vision to learn which current piece deserves more work.

Choose among continue, change, and stop. Then define what evidence will reopen the decision.

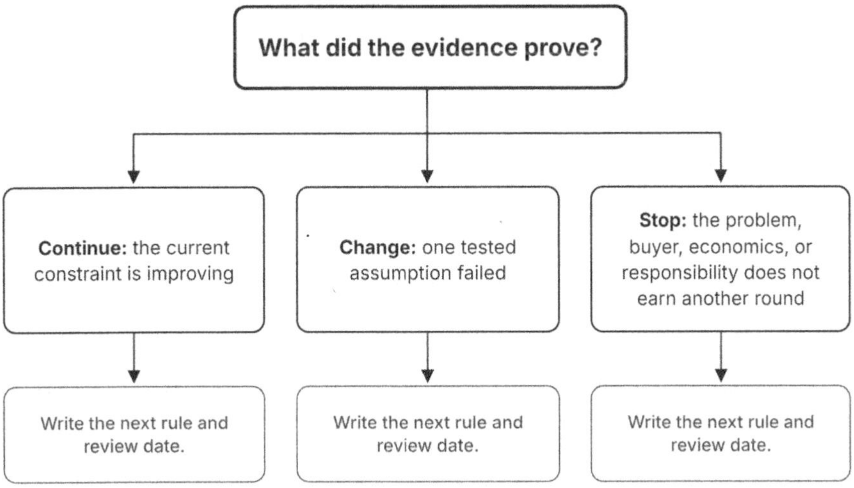

Your result is one **Founder Decision**.

Why It Matters

Many projects do not fail in one dramatic moment.

They continue without a rule.

The founder adds features because users requested them, changes the price after each conversation, shifts the audience when the offer is ignored, and calls every response learning. The project remains active but never becomes clearer.

A decision closes the current test.

Continue when the constraint is testable

Continue when:

- the problem still matters for a reachable audience;
- the product can deliver the bounded result;
- no trust blocker makes the test irresponsible;
- the economics have a plausible path; and
- one next experiment can reduce the current constraint.

Continue does not mean scale.

It means preserve the pieces that earned another test and change only what the evidence requires.

For example, if buyers use the product but setup takes too long, keep the product, audience, price, and promise while testing a simpler onboarding process.

Change when the current model is contradicted

Change when evidence points to a specific mismatch.

You may change:

- the first user or buyer;
- the broken moment;

- the Outcome Promise;
- the product boundary;
- the support package;
- the price;
- the buyer path; or
- the audience and channel.

Change one major assumption at a time when possible.

If you change the audience, promise, product, price, and channel together, the next result will not tell you what improved.

Return to the chapter that owns the contradicted decision. Do not patch a new feature onto a wrong promise.

Stop when responsibility exceeds evidence

Stopping can be the strongest business decision.

Stop when:

- the problem does not repeat or existing methods work well enough;
- the buyer cannot be reached or cannot act;
- the product cannot create the promised result responsibly;
- trust, legal, safety, or operational risk exceeds your current ability;
- delivery loses money with no plausible bounded fix;
- the work no longer fits the company or founder; or
- the next evidence would cost more than the decision is worth.

Stop does not erase what you learned. Preserve the brief, evidence, decision, and reusable work. Close live access, support, data, and payment obligations responsibly when they exist.

Find the smallest next experiment

The next experiment should target the current constraint from Chapter 19.

Use this sentence:

> *Keep ____________ unchanged. Change only ____________. Test it with ____________. Continue only if ____________ by ____________.*

Every blank matters.

Keep unchanged protects the evidence you already earned.

Change only names the hypothesis.

Test it with names an eligible audience and count.

Continue only if creates a measurable decision rule.

By adds a cutoff based on decisions, time, or both.

Use a decision rule, not a hope

"See how it goes" is not a decision rule.

A useful rule can include:

- a number of qualified offers;
- a number of purchases or explicit decisions;
- a maximum setup or support time;
- completion of the first product action;
- a trust or recovery requirement; or
- a date when the evidence will be read.

Keep the threshold proportional to the test. Four more qualified offers cannot establish a whole market. They can tell you whether a revised onboarding path deserves another cycle.

Name what the result cannot prove

Before running the next test, write the limit.

For example:

> *Two purchases from four qualified offers would support another bounded test of this offer. It would not prove broad demand, long-term use, or scalable acquisition.*

This sentence protects your future marketing and your future decisions.

Preserve responsibility through the handoff

A decision may create cleanup work.

If you continue, preserve support, data, buyer, and recovery obligations.

If you change, tell affected users what changes and what remains available.

If you stop, disable new purchases or invitations, deliver or refund outstanding commitments, provide the promised data-removal path, and retain only the information you are allowed and need to retain.

An AI agent can prepare a checklist. It should not perform live account, payment, deletion, outreach, or publication actions without explicit authorization and verification.

Record the decision where future work can find it

Do not leave the decision only in a chat transcript.

Place it beside the Build Brief and evidence. Include:

- the date;
- the current product and offer version;
- the evidence reviewed;
- the chosen decision;
- the current constraint;
- what stays unchanged;
- what changes;
- the cutoff and threshold;
- the owner; and
- the shutdown or recovery obligations.

Write the reason in plain language. A future builder should be able to understand the rule without reopening every transcript that led to it.

The next AI session should not have to guess which ideas were rejected or deferred.

Close the decision you are leaving

Founders often record the next idea and leave the current test half open.

Before starting another cycle, close five things:

1. save the evidence without rewriting it;
2. mark the product and offer version the evidence describes;
3. finish buyer, support, payment, and data obligations;
4. record deferred and rejected features with reasons; and
5. archive or stop any action that no longer belongs to the decision.

This creates a clean beginning for the next AI work order.

Distinguish a pause from a stop

A pause has a named reason and a condition for review.

```
Paused because:
No work will continue until:
Owner of the missing evidence or approval:
Review point:
```

A stop ends investment in the current product or offer. It may still require shutdown work.

Do not label an uncomfortable stop as a pause with no owner or review point. The project will continue consuming attention even while no evidence forms.

Do not label a temporary outside dependency as failure either. If the next step truly depends on a required approval, source, buyer decision, or safe technical review, pause it clearly and work only when the condition changes.

The decision is complete when both future work and current obligations have an honest state.

Practice Loop

Practice Loop has one constructed purchase, one week of initial use, a working product path, and positive contribution before fixed launch cost.

It also has weak buyer evidence and a delivery overrun. Setup and support take 55 minutes rather than the planned 45, reducing contribution from $24 to $19.

The case decision is:

Continue one bounded experiment.

Keep the product, adult hobby learner audience, Outcome Promise, Guided Setup offer, and $49 price unchanged.

Change only the onboarding checklist. The goal is to keep total preparation, setup, and support within 45 minutes per buyer without reducing the promised help. The 30-minute appointment remains part of that total, not a new 45-minute appointment.

Make the unchanged offer to four more qualified adult hobby learners.

Close invitations after those four contacts and allow seven days for responses after the last invitation. Complete the 14-day support window for each buyer before finalizing delivery cost.

Continue only if at least two of the four buy and each buyer's total delivery and support time stays within 45 minutes. Otherwise, change the offer or stop. A passing setup call alone does not pass the cost rule.

Even if that rule passes, the result will not prove broad demand, retention, scalable acquisition, or skill improvement. It will support one more business cycle with better delivery evidence.

The case does not add reminders, sync, accounts, or a teacher dashboard. Those requests do not address the current constraint.

Do It for Your App

Place the Problem Snapshot, Buyer Map, Evidence Decision, Build Brief, Working Path, Trust Map, Recovery Plan, Offer One-Pager, Buyer Path, Audience List, Launch Log, and Business Scorecard in front of you.

You do not need to reread every AI transcript. Read the decisions and proof.

Complete the Founder Decision:

```
DATE AND VERSION
What exact product and offer does this decision cover?

EVIDENCE REVIEWED
What observed behavior, decisions, payments, delivery, use, and
costs matter?

CURRENT CONSTRAINT
What one thing most limits the next result?

DECISION
Continue | Change | Stop

KEEP UNCHANGED
Which earned decisions remain fixed?

CHANGE ONLY
What one hypothesis will the next cycle test?

AUDIENCE AND CUTOFF
Who will face the test, how many decisions, and by when?

CONTINUE RULE
What result earns another cycle?

LIMIT
What will that result still not prove?

OWNER AND OBLIGATIONS
Who performs delivery, support, payment, data, recovery, and
shutdown work?
```

Ask the AI agent to challenge the logic without making the decision:

```
Review the Founder Decision against the supplied evidence and
current
constraint. Identify unsupported claims, changed variables hidden
inside the
experiment, thresholds that do not match the sample, obligations
without an
owner, and deferred features that have reentered scope. Do not
choose the
decision. Do not perform any live action.
```

Then decide.

If you continue, write the next Agent Work Order or offer test from the decision. If you change, return to the chapter that owns the changed assumption. If you stop, write and complete the shutdown checklist before beginning another project.

Do not reward the amount of work already spent. Reward the evidence and the fit with the business you want to run.

The app can be changed quickly. Your attention is the scarce resource.

Prove It

Your Founder Decision passes this chapter when:

- continue, change, or stop follows from the current constraint;
- the next test changes one major assumption;
- a measurable cutoff and continuation rule exist;
- the evidence limit and operational obligations are explicit; and
- the decision is stored where future work will find it.

Your Result

Save the **Founder Decision**.

Whether you kept the app or stopped after the evidence changed, you have a repeatable way to make the next decision. You can connect a broken moment, a product promise, an offer, and real evidence while AI handles the implementation work you approve.

Use the loop again only when the evidence earns another cycle.

Builder Toolkit and Next Steps

You reached a business decision with a working app, not just an idea.

Keep the decision and the evidence intact.

AI makes it easy to begin another build before the current test is understood. The best next step is usually not a fresh prompt. It is the action already written in the Founder Decision.

This toolkit helps you preserve the twenty results, hand the right context to an AI agent, route a new problem back to the right chapter, and run another bounded cycle without rebuilding the method from memory.

Open the Founder Decision First

Read the dated Founder Decision from Chapter 20 before changing the product, offer, audience, price, or launch path.

If the decision is **continue**, run the bounded experiment exactly as written. Hold every named item still. Change only the current constraint.

If the decision is **change**, return to the chapter that owns the contradicted assumption. Preserve enough of the prior test to understand what the change does.

If the decision is **stop**, close unsupported public actions through the authorized owner. Complete delivery, refund, support, access, and data obligations. Preserve the source, evidence, and reason.

If the project is **paused**, check the named restart condition. A pause with no condition, owner, or review point is an indefinite project.

Do not let an easy AI build replace the decision you already made.

Keep the Twenty Results Connected

The results form one decision chain. Each one answers a question the next result depends on.

Result	Question it answers	Reopen it when
Broken Moment	What keeps going wrong?	The observed friction changes.
Problem Snapshot	Who has this problem in a reachable situation?	The first user or current method changes.
Buyer Map	Who uses, pays, approves, and operates?	A new role or authority enters.
Evidence Decision	What evidence earns the next investment?	The rule fails or stronger counterevidence appears.
Outcome Promise	What one visible result matters?	Users cannot recognize or value the result.
Build Brief	What exact behavior may the agent implement?	Evidence changes the product decision.
Agent Work Order	How will the agent inspect, change, prove, and report?	Tool, risk, or project boundary changes.
Scope Box	What is inside now, manual, or later?	A new person, path, service, data type, or operation enters.
Working Path	Can one user reach one useful result and exit safely?	A main state or result changes.
Data Decision	What is forgotten, kept, shared, or deleted?	Persistence, account, sync, or new data enters.
Observation Note	What did a relevant person actually do?	Another test creates new behavior evidence.
Change Decision	Which one barrier deserves a bounded fix?	The retest fails or reveals an earlier wrong decision.
Trust Map	What can enter, stay, leave, act, and be claimed?	Data, access, public action, or responsibility expands.
Recovery Plan	How does the user return to safety?	A new failure or support burden appears.
Offer One-Pager	What exchange is the buyer choosing?	Buyer, promise, support, limit, or packaging changes.
Buyer Path	Can the person move from discovery through use and recovery?	A handoff, provider, delivery method, or owner changes.
Audience List	Who is eligible, reachable, and able to act?	The offer or channel changes.
Launch Log	What happened at each launch stage?	New authorized launch evidence arrives.

Result	Question it answers	Reopen it when
Business Scorecard	Which evidence lane is supported, mixed, unknown, or contradicted?	New actuals change the reading.
Founder Decision	What deserves the next unit of time or money?	The cutoff is reached or a stop condition occurs.

Do not rewrite an old result to make the new direction look inevitable.

Save a new version. Date the change. State which evidence caused it.

The chain should let a future reader answer:

- Why does this product exist?
- Who is it for?
- What is the product allowed to do?
- Which behavior has been proved?
- What can the business honestly claim?
- What is still unknown?
- Why is the next investment justified?

If those answers exist only in your memory, the project is not ready for another agent cycle.

Create a Clean Project Packet

Keep durable decisions near the project while storing private evidence separately.

A simple structure can look like this:

```
project/
  AGENTS.md
  PROJECT-INDEX.md
  BUILD-BRIEF.md
  BUILD-LOG.md
  decisions/
  evidence-references/
  source/
  tests/
  recovery/
```

The names can change. The jobs should remain clear.

Project instructions contain short durable rules the agent should follow every time.

Project index points to the current brief, current Founder Decision, current checkpoint, and authoritative evidence records.

Build Brief describes the approved product behavior for the current cycle.

Build Log records plans, changed files, checks, results, limits, and keep, revise, revert, or stop decisions.

Decision records preserve dated versions of the twenty results.

Evidence references point to approved source notes without copying unnecessary names, contact details, payment records, private messages, or sensitive information into the project.

Recovery records explain the known-good state and safe return method.

Use one obvious current version. An agent should not have to guess between `final`, `final-new`, and `final-really-new`.

When a record becomes historical, mark it superseded and point to the replacement. Do not delete the reason the product changed.

Use the Master Agent Handoff

The chapters use smaller prompts for individual moves. This handoff is the reusable starting point for a new approved cycle.

Replace the brackets with your current facts. Remove any line the task does not need.

```
CURRENT DECISION
Read [Founder Decision path] and [Business Scorecard path].
The current constraint is [one constraint].
Keep [named product, user, promise, offer, price, and boundary]
unchanged.
Change only [one approved hypothesis].

CURRENT PRODUCT
Read the project instructions, Project Index, Build Brief, Scope
Box,
Data Decision, Trust Map, Recovery Plan, current source, and tests.
Preserve unrelated and uncommitted work.

INSPECT
Do not edit yet.
Explain the current behavior, relevant files, conflicts,
assumptions,
trust implications, and known-good checkpoint.

PLAN
Propose the smallest change that tests the approved hypothesis.
List expected files, behavior changes, checks mapped to Done when,
regression checks, evidence to record, and exact revert path.

PAUSE BEFORE
A new user, buyer, promise, feature, dependency, service, account,
network action, data type, credential, payment, public action,
message,
spending, destructive operation, or change outside the approved
scope.

IMPLEMENT
After plan approval, create the checkpoint and implement only the
plan.
Do not publish, send, charge, spend, enroll, or change a live
account.

PROVE
Run the focused checks and the complete Working Path.
Test the affected data, trust, accessibility, failure, recovery,
and
buyer behavior at the level of responsibility this change creates.

REPORT
Return the behavior, files changed, checks and exact results,
failed or
unproven items, assumptions, limits, recovery path, and deferred
work.
Do not choose the founder's final decision.
```

Review the inspection before the plan. Review the plan before implementation. Review the actual behavior and changed files before keeping the result.

The handoff is not permission to perform every line. The agent still stops at the named approval boundaries.

If the task is small, shorten the handoff. Keep the current decision, relevant context, boundary, proof, and report. Repeated decoration does not make an agent safer.

Match Proof to Responsibility

Every change needs evidence. Higher-responsibility changes need deeper evidence.

Local, reversible behavior

Examples include a label, layout, local form, or a small path using non-sensitive test data.

Proof can include:

- mapped behavior checks;
- the full Working Path;
- blank, long, repeat, reset, and phone-sized states;
- changed-file review; and
- a tested checkpoint.

Persistent or public behavior

Examples include local saved data, a public preview, an external request, user-generated content, or a maintained host.

Add:

- storage, refresh, deletion, and recovery tests;
- network and dependency inspection;
- plain-language disclosure;
- accessibility review appropriate to the path;
- public-claim review; and
- an authorized owner for publication and support.

High-responsibility behavior

Examples include identity, authentication, private records, payment, file uploads, provider callbacks, administrative actions, youth data, or health, financial, legal, employment, or safety consequences.

Stop the beginner workflow and bring in deeper architecture, security, privacy, accessibility, legal, financial, or domain review as appropriate.

Use maintained providers for sensitive functions. Keep secrets out of browser code, project files, prompts, screenshots, and ordinary logs.

Passing a test does not prove that the product is safe, legal, accessible, or viable for every user. It proves the behavior covered by that test in the state you tested.

Improve the Constraint, Not the Feature List

Return to the current constraint in the Business Scorecard.

When the audience was not reached, improve the approved path to eligible buyers. Do not rebuild the interface.

When eligible people were reached but did not reply, inspect the invitation, channel, timing, relevance, and broken moment. Silence does not choose the cause.

When buyers do not understand the offer, improve the buyer moment, result, included help, limits, and next action. Do not hide the price or add unrelated bonuses.

When qualified buyers understand and decline, revisit the problem, buyer, offer, or price. Keep product polish out of the first diagnosis.

When buyers pay but cannot create the Outcome Promise, return to the Working Path, observation, and trust work.

When buyers receive the product but do not begin, inspect delivery, onboarding, first use, and expectation.

When delivery takes too long, improve the checklist, product path, or support boundary. Track all time again.

When contribution is negative, separate price, variable cost, delivery labor, and fixed work before choosing the change.

When a trust, safety, or legal issue appears, stop the affected live use until qualified review closes it.

Use this routing table:

Current problem	Return first to
The broken moment no longer repeats	Chapters 1 and 2
User, buyer, or approval is wrong	Chapter 3
Evidence did not earn the build	Chapter 4
Result is unclear or uncontrollable	Chapter 5
Agent is building the wrong behavior	Chapters 6 and 7
Another product entered scope	Chapter 8
User cannot finish the path	Chapter 9
Memory or account expectation is wrong	Chapter 10
You do not know where use breaks	Chapter 11
The last fix did not remove the barrier	Chapter 12
Data, access, action, or claim is unsafe	Chapter 13
Failure has no safe next step	Chapter 14
Buyer misunderstands the exchange	Chapter 15
Payment, delivery, use, or support handoff fails	Chapter 16
Audience cannot be qualified or reached	Chapter 17
Launch states or obligations are unclear	Chapter 18
The evidence story exceeds the facts	Chapter 19
The project continues without a rule	Chapter 20

One constraint keeps the next test readable. Other unknowns remain visible. They do not all enter the next build.

Keep the Next Experiment Readable

Write the experiment in one sentence:

> *Keep ____________ unchanged. Change only ____________. Test it with ____________. Continue only if ____________ by ____________.*

Then add the limit:

> *Even if this passes, it will not prove ____________.*

Check the experiment against five rules.

1. **One current constraint:** the Business Scorecard identifies the reason for the test.
2. **One major variable:** audience, promise, product, price, offer, channel, or delivery does not change silently with another.
3. **One eligible group:** the people facing the test match the Audience List.
4. **One cutoff:** a number of decisions, amount of time, spending limit, or date ends the cycle.
5. **One pass and fail action:** both outcomes lead to a written next decision.

Do not move the threshold after the result arrives merely to continue the project.

Do stop early for a false claim, broken delivery, trust failure, missing authorization, responsibility you cannot own, or harm that should not be repeated.

Add Deeper Skills When the Product Needs Them

This book keeps implementation light on purpose. Your next product may earn a deeper technical or operating skill.

Learn the skill when it solves a demonstrated need.

Version control helps you compare changes, preserve branches of work, and return to known states. Add it when verified folder copies no longer provide enough recovery.

Automated tests repeat important checks without relying on memory. Add them around behavior that has broken, handles meaningful data, controls access, or changes often.

Accessibility review goes beyond the bounded keyboard, focus, text, and phone-sized checks in this book. Bring in deeper testing when the audience, product, or public obligation requires it.

Server-side development supports accounts, protected secrets, shared data, provider callbacks, and controlled administrative behavior. It also creates new security, privacy, reliability, recovery, and cost responsibilities.

Databases support durable and shared records. They require a data model, access control, backup, retention, deletion, migration, monitoring, and recovery decisions.

Security review becomes deeper as the product handles identity, authorization, sensitive data, money, external files, untrusted content, process execution, provider callbacks, or privileged actions.

Product analytics can answer behavior questions at larger scale. It also creates consent, disclosure, retention, interpretation, and data-minimization decisions. Do not add hidden tracking merely because a dashboard is available.

Business operations include bookkeeping, taxes, refunds, disputes, customer records, contracts, support commitments, accessibility obligations, and provider terms. Use qualified help when the consequence exceeds a learning exercise.

Marketing and sales systems can increase reach. Add them after the first audience and message are clear enough that more reach will produce readable evidence rather than more noise.

Do not study or build all of these at once. Choose the one connected to the current constraint and responsibility.

Keep AI Inside a Clear Role

Use AI for work it can make faster and easier to review:

- inspect the current project;
- locate the source of truth;

- draft a bounded plan;
- implement approved behavior;
- run repeatable checks;
- explain changed files;
- maintain the build record;
- reconcile counts and arithmetic;
- compare evidence with a claim; and
- challenge unsupported conclusions.

Keep human control over:

- which problem matters;
- who the user and buyer are;
- which evidence is real;
- which permission is granted;
- which risk is acceptable;
- which claim becomes public;
- which offer is made;
- how much time or money to invest;
- whether a live action is authorized; and
- whether to keep, revise, revert, stop, continue, or change.

The agent's speed is useful only inside that boundary.

Preserve the Youth and Group Boundary

The retail book is for a general audience. A high-school cohort can use the same method through a more controlled operating path.

An approved adult owns live accounts, outside contact, payment, refunds, public communication, and publication for an under-18 builder. The student can still own the problem, product direction, observation, evidence reading, and founder decision.

When live action is not approved, use a local build, test mode, inquiry rehearsal, assigned role, or clearly labeled scenario. Do not report a rehearsal as a launch, commitment, customer, or sale.

Schools, companies, clubs, and other groups may add their own approval and data rules. Required approval is part of the product boundary, not an obstacle to work around.

Reuse the Method

The next app may use a different technology, buyer, or business model. The Builder Loop still applies.

Observe behavior before defining the result. Give the agent a brief instead of a wish. Prove the changed behavior instead of accepting a completion message.

Watch a relevant person act. Ask a qualified buyer to decide. Record the result separately from your interpretation.

Then make the next choice before starting the next build.

The method should become familiar. The evidence should remain specific to each product.

Current Guidance Used in This Edition

Tools and standards change. The body emphasizes durable behavior. These primary sources support the maintained technical guidance in this edition:

- OpenAI Codex prompting guidance for goals, context, constraints, durable instructions, review, and verification: https://learn.chatgpt.com/docs/prompting
- OpenAI guidance for durable `AGENTS.md` project instructions: https://learn.chatgpt.com/docs/agent-configuration/agents-md
- OpenAI Codex approvals and security guidance: https://learn.chatgpt.com/docs/agent-approvals-security
- MDN local-storage documentation for browser persistence and its limits: https://developer.mozilla.org/en-US/docs/Web/API/Window/localStorage

- W3C Web Content Accessibility Guidelines 2.2: https://www.w3.org/TR/WCAG22/
- OWASP HTML5 Security Cheat Sheet for local-storage and browser-data safeguards: https://cheatsheetseries.owasp.org/cheatsheets/HTML5_Security_Cheat_Sheet.html
- OWASP DOM based XSS Prevention Cheat Sheet for displaying user-controlled text safely: https://cheatsheetseries.owasp.org/cheatsheets/DOM_based_XSS_Prevention_Cheat_Sheet.html
- Stripe Payment Links as one hosted-payment example: https://docs.stripe.com/payment-links/create
- Stripe Checkout documentation: https://docs.stripe.com/payments/checkout
- Stripe secret-key guidance: https://docs.stripe.com/keys-best-practices

Verify the latest official source before relying on a named product, provider, fee, term, account path, or legal obligation.

Make the Next Decision Visible

Put the next decision date or completed-test point somewhere you will see it.

When that point arrives, open the evidence before opening the code.

Build only after the decision earns another build.

Keep Building with unQbd

You finished a real product path and a repeatable way to decide what it needs next.

Continue learning with practical books across software, AI, business, fiction, and family reading on unQbd.

QR destination: https://unqbd.com/app

Explore the current reading and membership options at https://unqbd.com/app.

If you are under 18, an approved adult must review any account, subscription, payment, public review, outside contact, or publication.

If this book helped you make a clearer build or business decision, an honest review can help another reader decide whether it fits them.

Thank you for reading.

www.ingramcontent.com/pod-product-compliance
Lightning Source LLC
LaVergne TN
LVHW060546061126
851857LV00017B/1916